Semantics and language analysis

THE BOBBS-MERRILL SERIES IN *Speech Communication*

RUSSEL R. WINDES, *Editor*

ROBERT L. BENJAMIN

Semantics and language analysis

The Bobbs-Merrill Company, Inc.
INDIANAPOLIS AND NEW YORK

P325
B4
cop.2

Editor's foreword

The 1930s were times of intense intellectual confrontation in America, times when slogans like "class conflict," "rule of the proletariat," "social planning," and "cooperative society," rang out against traditional shibboleths like "free enterprise," "the better people," "survival of the fittest," and "education and hard work—the best way to get ahead." In this period of intellectual certainty among adherents of competing social philosophies, Max Lerner not surprisingly wrote in 1939 that ideas were "weapons" in the personal struggles each individual has for the resolution of his tensions, and "in the struggles for power and order that every age has and every culture."

If we accept the proposition that ideas are weapons, then even textbooks, derivative though they may be, come to have significance as statements of position in intellectual conflict. Many special interest groups have so regarded them. Shall a government textbook favor public utilities? This question engrossed the energies of private utility lobbyists for years. Shall the Negro be depicted in history books as a willing slave or as a restive man under a brutalizing system? That question will vex curriculum committees for years. Textbooks, then, document the struggles and preoccupations of their times. This fact is true of the semantics textbooks used in college classrooms no less than of other books.

As documents in intellectual history, semantics books can be perceived and analyzed from a number of points of view. In this short compass let me emphasize a single theme of previous works in semantics: They display an orientation which can be diffusely labeled, "The Progressive Inclination." The argument underlying these books goes something like this: If only people **thought** straight, we could make important, beneficial changes in our social institutions. But people cannot think straight if they continually abuse their language. If language could only be made to represent reality, then reality could be diagnosed and altered.

From this general orientation or predisposition have arisen at least four definable types of writers of semantics books. First is the "inside dopester." As the naïve freshmen enter State University this writer tells them that words like God and Motherhood, chastity and truth, really don't mean anything. This information the students carry home on their Thanksgiving holiday, and by Friday night everyone in the family is seriously disturbed.

Allied to the "inside dopester" is the "campus Socrates," the teacher of wisdom. This writer brings into question all the "old certainties" on the basis that language can never express a certain truth.

Both the "inside dopester" and the "campus Socrates" have a friend in the form of the "amateur psychiatrist" who sees language as a series of examples of "communication pathologies." He argues in his book that human relations are based on communication, and most communication is hopelessly muddled by the inability of language accurately to transfer meaning.

The "instrumental idealist" takes heart from the language pathologist. He argues the corollary that, if only language can be improved, then the world can be improved. The instrumental idealists come in two variants: those who think that rules of language as a tool for social and psychological betterment have already been discovered and need only to be applied; those who hope that theoreticians can soon hand down the guidelines of a language proper for social reconstruction.

Of course, the observations and caricatures above are exaggerated and even flippant. With equal certainty many writers and teachers of semantics have been misrepresented. But if these tendencies, described above, have been a part of the semantic heritage, then we should seriously question the approach that has been taken. Are not students today rather sophisticated about much of the meaninglessness which people "over thirty" pass off as wisdom? If they are, isn't there the need to point out that much language is meaningful. The reaction to a conviction of the meaninglessness of language might just as often be the extravagant, demagogic use of language. In the same sense, the teacher of wisdom, the amateur psychologist, and the instrumental idealist often have only a negative sort of analysis to make, since we do not have today, as we did in the past, the calming assurance that the **positive government** or **real human understanding** are answers to social and personal problems.

In Professor Benjamin's presentation, **semantics** is not a method which deals with the establishment of truth about the world. Rather, semantics is a study of an extremely complex and indispensable agent of human interaction. Professor Benjamin places emphasis on the instances of effective communication of meaning, as well as the failures to communicate well. He places less emphasis on whether individuals are communicating a picture of the real world, than on whether people are communicating the world as they perceive it. In the author's words, "our investigation (of semantics) ends where verification begins." Professor Benjamin's book, stressing as it does the operation of language as a coherent system, may provide a useful anodyne to those texts which stress the traditional but still premature expectation that language analysis is the source of wisdom, psychological help and social melioration.

Professor Benjamin's approach to semantics is essentially positive. He starts by assuming that language works rather well most of the time; that learning **how** it works (its eccentricities and limitations) can profit the student far more than intensive perusal of communication breakdowns. The book, therefore, begins with language, not in isolated word segments, but in the way the individual consumes and produces it—in mixed bunches of assertions, questions, metaphors and ejaculations which often say more about the author than the subject matter. With the case study, "Get Tough," the student is exposed successively to various aspects of the meaning-analysis of language, always with the emphasis on **finding** and **classifying** meaning. The communicators are assumed innocent until proven guilty. Meaning is there, though it may be of a different kind than expected.

Professor Benjamin does not expect the reader to revolutionize his language habits overnight. He believes semantics will cause the student to **think differently** about his language; in the end the student may be using the same words, only with far greater insight. Perhaps words from the concluding chapter might best summarize the opportunities of this volume, ". . . your language will be ready—when you are."

Russel R. Windes

Contents

Conclusion   99

Introduction

Students of communication are often asked to imagine a world without language, a world in which things and people exist and transactions take place all without communication. People pass, work together, fight among themselves, but always like passing shadows with no words spoken among them. The thoughts, dreams, and passions of the people of this world may find release in deeds, but never in words.

Such a world is indeed strange to contemplate. But equally fascinating is the reverse idea of a world full of language as we know it today, but one in which the things talked about are strangely absent. One must take a moment to erase an obvious self-contradiction in such a world. First, there could be no language without people to speak it or write it and others to listen and read. So even as we imagine a language without an object-world, part of this world—the producers and consumers of the language—must creep back in. But more important, what would be the purpose of language without a world to talk about? Language is **about** the world. A language about nothing is inconceivable.

But is language—all of it—really about the world? Take any sentence from any book near your hand—this book, perhaps—and try to make links word-by-word to the world outside. What happens to words like "the," "only," "but," and "immeasurable"? When in our fancy we tried to take from language the world it was about, we didn't seem to do much damage. Like the grin without the cat, language goes on and on, seeming somehow to hang together and make sense, even though many of its separate parts are manifestly about nothing. If this is the language we are counting on to save the world from itself—or from us—some serious study is plainly in order. And as a student of communication you deserve a close look at your language. This book will provide that close look.

A meaning approach to language

But how are we to approach anything so intricate and complex as language? Our language-without-the-world fantasy illustrated only one of these intricacies: the fact that many words do not **by themselves** refer to the world. Semantics—the study of **how language means**— can lay bare for us many more facets of the linguistic instruments. But if we fail to keep a constant perspective, semantics can become the tail that wags the dog. Perhaps our best procedure is to make note of some typical Loreleis of semantic study, and set a course to avoid them.

The demon hypothesis.   One cannot read even casually the literature of the past half-century in the field of semantics without groaning under the oppressive weight of actual or impending breakdown. Communication, we are told, comes apart constantly. What I say to you has little or no chance of reaching you unimpaired; and even if it does, you will somehow perceive it awry. What I send will bear little resemblance to what you receive; an invisible demon is always there to confound my meanings. And even if my words by some miracle get through with meaning intact, the world I perceived as I spoke will have changed in the interim[1] and what I said doesn't fit any more.

Certainly a thorough study of the causes of communication breakdown is both necessary and worthwhile. But in the process I fear we lose sight of the remarkable fact that **language works.** And work it does, in strange and wonderful ways, conveying incredible nuance side by side with precise scientific accuracy; couching, sometimes even hiding, our own confusion and uncertainty, even displaying a semblance of order and sanity while we get our scrambled thoughts in shape. The following chapters will stress **how** language works: the many ways in which it can be meaningful. The question of what happens when (like any other tool) language is abused, will be subordinated to a study of its proper and successful uses.

[1] S. I. Hayakawa, **Language in Thought and Action**, 2nd. ed. (New York: Harcourt, Brace and World, 1964), p. 240.

The word hypothesis. A second trend in modern language study has placed great stress on words. If you have read in the field of general semantics you probably have been impressed with the many examples of individual words which cause meaning troubles. Dictionaries define words; rarely long phrases. Recent developments in psycholinguistics have also placed stress on the single word, with occasional sojourns into two-word combinations.[2] It was not until the British "Ordinary Language" approach began to creep into this country that larger units of language—sentences and paragraphs—began to get their fair share of attention.

In this book you will be asked to look first at communication the way we produce and consume it—in wholesale, heterogeneous masses. After all, in the give-and-take of everyday discourse you will rarely have a chance to weigh a word at a time. Later you will look at smaller units—sentences—and study the internal components of these sentences—words and phrases. In this way the important and necessary findings of modern word researchers may be subordinated to your need to understand language as you are forced to perceive it and use it: in a complex which includes environmental variables, oral nuance, human error—and more language.

The spectator hypothesis. A third fad in communication analysis is the view of the spectator. The who-says-what-to-whom approach has led many modern analysts to sit on the sidelines and watch while one source produces communication and others consume and react.

While much can be learned from the sidelines, you have the role of **producer** and **consumer** of communication. While the spectator describes reaction to a given communication, you as the consumer are trying to decide how you **should** react. Likewise as a producer you will want to be able to predict in advance what reception and reaction your language will provoke. In this book you will be asked alternately to regard language as coming **from** you or **at** you, never merely passing by.

The truth-is-king hypothesis. A fourth trend among modern language experts, particularly those who deal with propaganda analysis, is preoccupation with **truth**.[3] Although most analysts pay lip-service to

---

[2] Osgood, Charles E.; Suci, George J.; and Tannenbaum, Percy H., **The Measurement of Meaning** (Urbana, Ill.: University of Illinois Press, 1957), *passim*, chap. i, iii.
[3] Consider, for example, current "Truth in Advertising" and "Truth in Packaging" campaigns.

the importance of meaning, they nevertheless spend most of their time detecting and exposing errors in factual reporting or in reasoning. But completely aside from the tendencies among experts, there can be little doubt about the layman's instinctive reaction to the claims about the world: He will surely challenge truth before he thinks to question meaning.

Our approach in the following pages will be based on what seems to be a self-evident assumption: that it makes little sense to challenge the veracity of an assertion one doesn't understand. Thus in the overall scheme of things we place no lesser emphasis on truth than does its most avid guardian; we insist only that meaning come first.

Further—as a kind of boundary to our efforts—we shall make sure that our investigation **ends** where verification **begins.** That is, once we have satisfied ourselves—as producers or consumers of communication—that meaning problems have been taken care of, then our concern as semanticists shall be said to be ended.

One final observation about a common misconception regarding semantics: that every comment about meaning in someones' communication is necessarily some kind of insult. Somehow semantics has become erroneously identified with meaning-**denial.** Throughout our studies here the communicator will always be assumed innocent until proven guilty. As a communication consumer you will be expected to assume that meaning **is there;** that it has only to be located. As a producer, of course, you will hopefully use semantic understanding as a means, not to narrow, but to widen the bands of communication which link you to your fellow man.

Semantics and the communicator

Whether your special interest is informal communication—conversation, interviewing, group discussion—or more formal situations—platform speaking or debating—you are sure to spend many of your waking hours as a consumer or producer of discourse. To understand the impact of semantic awareness on your communication habits and skills, you need to see yourself in each of these two roles.

You as consumer.   To those who look to this book for help in language production—toward better speaking and writing—its apparent preoccupation with the consumer of discourse may seem disconcerting. Indeed, language analysis has for the consumer a value quite apart from better production: It helps provide a selective shield against today's verbal onslaught. Your wallet is fatter than your great-grandfather's, and more discoursers than ever before aim to part you from its contents. Producers of language will also want your vote, your strong back, maybe your life. If you fail to look sharply at their wares —and semantics will help you look—they may in the end have their way with you.

You as producer. If, however, higher quality production is your goal, you will find that rigorous study of the other fellow's communication will alert you to your own language habits, perhaps improve them. This book will also expose you to the immense variety of linguistic forms. But you are not expected to revolutionize your communication just because you've discovered some disquieting facts about your prior language habits. And even if, in the end, you find yourself speaking and writing much as you did before, you will at least be doing so with a fuller realization of what you are about. And that is something.

Semantics
and language
analysis

ONE

Language and the world

GET TOUGH—OR GIVE UP!

America is coming to a crossroads. Those who are bent on destroying our country by senseless rioting, looting, and vandalism have forced us to a point where we must protect what is left. The minority menace, forsaking the system which gave it freedom, has challenged the very roots of democracy. Can we afford to ignore this challenge?

Where is the justice in the minority axe? Where is the justice in "Give-us-what-we-want-or-else"?

Of course minorities have their grievances, and these must be expressed —but only at the ballot box! This is what democracy means. It means minorities convincing majorities that they are wrong. It means qualifying for jobs—not demanding them. It means earning the right to respectable housing, and learning to keep it respectable—not interfering with our God-given right to choose our own neighbors!

Surely the Great Creator, in blessing this land above all others, did not intend it to fall before the looter's larrup or the blackguard's blackjack. Law and order made this nation—let us not abandon it to a handful of thugs.

But even as the "liberals" stand by and cheer, the thugs are getting tough. We too must get tough—or give up.

In the introduction you were told that we produce and consume communication not a word at a time, but in large jumbles. The foregoing is an example—hopefully not typical—of such discourse. Study the passage for a moment, pretending it is a speech you have just heard or an editorial you read in yesterday's newspaper. Forget the subject matter and your possible reactions to the author's position, and concentrate on the language itself. Your first reaction may be: "It's loaded!" But what is it about this discourse that makes it loaded? What kinds of devices—deliberate or inadvertent—can you point out?

You probably first wondered how you were to react to those references to God and the Great Creator. Maybe you resented having religious names and concepts thrust into what is obviously a social argument. Perhaps next, such phrases as "minority axe" and "looter's larrup" drew your attention. (Surely the author was not referring literally to axes and larrups.) You may also have noticed near the beginning a series of questions. How is one to react to questions in the middle of an argument? And what about the quotation marks around the word "liberals"? Is the author indicating some special meaning here? These features should have been immediately apparent. And, to the linguistically sophisticated, "forced" and "right" may have flashed a warning signal.

If your immediate reaction to this verbal barrage was to toss it over your shoulder and forget about it, take another look. A quick glance at one of your old favorites—a speech or essay you wrote—will probably reveal many of the same devices. One should note here that to comment on the variety of ways in which a communicator expresses himself is not to condemn or deride, but to emphasize that **language may be meaningful in more than one way.** Behind the massive onslaught of the "Get Tough" passage something very important may have been said or intended. Surely if we are to do justice to this author—or to any other producer of communication—some kind of systematic appraisal is in order. As tempting as it may be at this point to sail into the "Get Tough" passage, in doing so we should be getting ahead of ourselves. We are in no position even to delineate the kinds of meaning in the passage, let alone criticize their use, until we establish what we want to mean by "linguistic meaning." We must, that is, take a quick look at the **nature** of language and the way it talks about the world.

How language works

The easiest way to look at language in operation is to focus for a moment on the things, people, and transactions that language talks about. You will remember from the introduction that semantics deals with the links between language and the world. With this in mind you might expect language to be built in two parts. The first part would comprise the names of all the things we want to talk about, and the second part would be the machinery for saying-**about** these things. But when we look at the structure of English (the only language available to us at the moment) we find, not an orderly set of names of things side by side with another orderly set of symbols for talking about these things, but rather a disorderly complex of words and phrases with only the most cursory instructions as to how to use them. And if I start to name some simple things, such as the tall man standing on my patio with a briefcase in his hand, I find it takes thirteen words just to name what I want to talk about—and I still haven't said anything about him! (For we say with verbs, and no verb is present in that thirteen-word phrase.) To be sure, most of the things we talk about can be named in fewer than thirteen words—but some take many more!

What is there about the nature of language—or the nature of the world—which makes the linguistic connection so awkward and its process so complicated? Why hasn't language jiggled itself down to a one-to-one correlation with the outside world? Answers to these questions lie in part in the nature of symbolism itself. Without purporting to explore this exciting science in any depth we must nevertheless look at symbolism and its relation to language.

What is a symbol? A symbol is anything that stands for something else. Let us ignore for a moment that remarkable human ability which enables us to look at a symbol and think about its object. Let us rather concentrate on the symbol itself. Two observations are immediately important.

A. Being a symbol may be a part-time job.

Anything may become a symbol overnight; and any symbol may lose its symbolic nature through agreement, obsolescence or neglect. Is an eagle a symbol or a bird? In this country it is both. The fact that the eagle functions as a living part of our world does not prevent it from being a symbol of a nation (or its government or way of life). Furthermore, suppose by unanimous consent we abolish the eagle as our national symbol and substitute the oak tree. Depending on the completeness of agreement, the eagle has ceased being a symbol and the oak has become one. This suddenness of transformation becomes more vivid when one visualizes the use of codes in wartime. A given code, successful for a time, becomes obsolete due to exposure and a new code replaces it. All members of the using community are notified, and immediately an organized system of symbols which yesterday controlled millions of lives becomes junk; and what a moment ago would have been a pile of pointless marks and scratches takes on in a twinkling the powerful thrust of significance.

B. A symbol has no set shape, size or characteristic.

What do an eagle, a piece of colored cloth, an articulated noise and some scratches on a paper have in common? Only the fact that by common agreement they may stand for something besides themselves. This makes them symbols. Clearly their physical configuration has no bearing on their capacity to symbolize. Their success or failure as symbols depends on three factors: **definiteness, consistency** and **universality.**

Definiteness.   What is it for a symbol to be definite? If I point to a work bench with an assortment of tools on it and say, "Hand me the tool," I'm likely to get almost anything. Clearly in this context "tool" is not definite enough to make the symbol work. If on the other hand I say, "Hand me the wrench," the symbol "wrench" should in normal circumstances get me what I want. If, however, the bench contains a variety of wrenches I may need to be even more specific. The point is that the symbol needs to be as definite as the situation requires.

Such a criterion would seem easy to identify and adhere to. But the world is unhappily not as definite as our symbols suggest. Take the concept indicated by the symbol "color-blind."[1] Every day scores of persons applying for driving licenses are asked to sort out bits of colored yarn, or perform some other kind of test, as a result of which they are classified as color-blind or not. This classification is usually noted on the license. But what happens when we increase the number of yarn bits and make the distinction between colors more difficult to determine? Some who passed the test before will now fail; and more persons will be added to the "color-blind" list. Thus a symbol which appeared on the surface to be comfortably definite is found on careful examination to have fuzzy edges.

Further analysis will show us, however, that it is the world—not the symbol—that has the fuzzy edge. The term "color-blind" is indefinite only because the people and properties it talks about do not exactly fall into categories. In short, this symbol is as definite as it needs to be to

[1] Max Black, **Language and Philosophy: Studies in Method** (Ithaca, N. Y.: Cornell University Press, 1949), chap. ii and *passim.*

serve the context in which it is used: namely, to distinguish those drivers who can read certain signals from those who can't. If a new context (e.g., interior decorating) demands a more precise distinction, a new symbolic structure will have to be erected.

Consistency. A symbol is consistent to the extent that it hangs on to its meanings throughout its use in a given discourse. The practice of allowing (or causing) a symbol to waiver from one use to the next— a process sometimes called **equivocation**—may conveniently permit one to move from the undeniable to the highly unlikely, often with logical impunity. Consider the following argument.

> In any enterprise, management is responsible for the care and maintenance of the means of production.
>
> The workers are a part of the means of production.
>
> Therefore, management is responsible for the care and maintenance of the workers.

It doesn't take much effort for one to see what has happened in the course of this argument. The term "means of production," which originally meant (1) machinery and equipment, was shifted in the second sentence to include (2) anything necessary to run the business. Some of us who accepted the first statement under meaning (1) might be unwilling to accept it under meaning (2). Logicians classify this shift of meaning in the course of a deductive argument as "the fourth-term fallacy."

The criterion of consistency in symbolic reference is most sharply illustrated in a special form of the parlor game "Twenty Questions," a pastime in which most of us have indulged under one name or another. In this game one person leaves the room while the remaining group decides upon an object unknown to the absentee. When the latter returns he is permitted to ask a series of yes-or-no questions about the unknown object (e.g., "is it mineral?") until he is able to produce its name. The next time you find yourself engaged in this popular pastime, insist that the participants get in a circle, and that the guesser ask his questions alternately of the persons around him. Then when a new guesser has left the room—preferably one who fancies himself rather good at the game—introduce (as "it") "the left shoe of the person just to the right of the one who is being asked the question at the moment." As the questioning develops the answers will seem to contradict one another due to the fact that "it" refers to something different each time an answer is given. After the game is up and the trick revealed, ask the questioner how he felt when he started getting answers which he regarded as contradictory. Most people describe a sense of disbelief and disorientation as they feel the comfortable ground of logical consistency slipping from beneath them. Unfortunately, in the heat of everyday discourse this healthy demand for consistent symbolism is not widely practiced. Many symbols sneak through the bonds of consistency and are allowed to slip and weasel their way from one meaning to another.

Universality.   It is clearly of no avail to make our symbolic system definite and consistent if only some of us are agreed to it. One need only visualize a society in which half the community interpreted "stop" as a directive to proceed at full speed, to see the chaos that would result from lack of universality. For a symbolic system to work properly every member of the using community must not only understand but agree to the connections between most symbols and their objects. The constant need to keep a linguistic system universal is a problem of **definition,** which is treated in detail in a future chapter.

So far we have been talking about symbols and their objects as though the connections were arbitrary and pre-planned. Experience and linguistic history would seem to contradict this assumption. Surely words like "hiss," "bang," and "clang" have natural ties to the sounds they name, and to use the word "hiss" for a groan would seem most unnatural. It should be noted, however, that this linguistic phenomenon—called onomatopoeia—is psychophysical and not logically necessary.

But the argument does not stop here. Roger Brown cites interlingual studies which suggest that many other symbols are tied to their objects in ways which are not purely arbitrary.[2] If words do not belong to things by nature, why is the word "umbulolo" such a good word for a mound or swelling?

Students of Plato will recognize this controversy as being thousands of years old. Fortunately we don't have to embroil ourselves in this now. All we need to agree to is that there is no **necessary logical connection** between a thing and its name. Once this has been accepted, the criteria of definiteness, consistency and universality become established; and we are ready to look at language.

---

[2] Roger Brown, **Words and Things** (Glencoe, Ill.: The Free Press, 1958), chap. iv.

What makes a language? So far we have referred casually to "linguistic systems" without specifying what these are. It is time now to focus on language itself. A language may be defined as an organized set of symbols with explicit or implicit rules of syntax. (By "syntax" we mean the way the symbols go together.) It follows immediately that the three-fold definite-consistent-universal requirement predicated originally of symbols, is also a requirement of language.

If you have been following closely, you probably noticed that the foregoing definition of "language" automatically excludes certain symbols. What happens, for example, to the eagle and the flag? Surely they are symbols, as they stand for something other than themselves. But equally surely they are not a part of any language.[3] To make the distinction clear, the term **"linguistic symbol"** will be used to refer to symbols which are parts of a language (essentially the words appearing in dictionaries). Such items as flags and eagles are called "non-linguistic symbols." The latter, while admittedly complex and fascinating, are not a part of our subject.

A. **Primary and secondary languages.** An important distinction must now be made as follows:

> Primary language: A language whose symbols stand directly for the world talked about.

> Secondary language: A language which for necessity, convenience or amusement is devised to represent another language.

English, Hebrew, Tagalog, and some sign languages are primary languages. Their symbols refer directly to the world their users wish to talk about. Morse code, shorthand and Braille are secondary languages; they substitute for another language.

B. **Are all written languages secondary?** Inasmuch as written languages presumably developed after their oral counterparts, they ought rightly to be regarded as secondary. In practice, however, oral and written languages have existed side by side so long that they are treated as merely two ways to formulate one language. Thus, spoken and written English are considered not as a primary and secondary language but as one primary language. Both formulations (oral and written) are said to refer directly to the world the language is about.

---

[3] Do not confuse the **name** "flag," which is, of course, part of a language, with a flag itself, which is not.

Talking about language

Throughout this book we shall be talking mostly about language. To do this we ought to have a special set of tools equipped to deal with language itself rather than with the non-linguistic world. (Although a pair of pliers may be useful to handle a great variety of metallic items, we would never expect the pliers to pick themselves up.) Unfortunately, English, in its abject poverty, gives us no such tools. If we want to talk about language, we are told in effect we must use for this talking the very language we talk about! Such a paradox leads to questions like these: When I say "chair" do I mean the sound I made or a piece of furniture? When I write "the word puzzle is interesting" am I talking about the six-letter word "puzzle" or a game played with words?

Linguistic experts, in developing systems (parallel to our cultural language) which purport to be relatively free from vagueness and ambiguity, usually devise a separate set of symbols with a separate set of rules for talking about their language. This separate set they call "meta-language," a language about language. We could do the same for English. But instead of becoming involved in the complex job of constructing a new set of linguistic machinery, it is suggested that we reexamine English for a meta-linguistic principle that will see us through. Two factors are immediately evident:

1. The English language functions (as do most other languages) as its own meta-language. Such words as "word," "sentence," "paragraph," designate general classes of language units. But there is no universal, consistent way of referring to a specific piece of language without danger of confusing the reference with whatever the piece of language is about.

2. Most of us—knowingly or instinctively—leave some of our discourse as vague as possible, especially when dealing with high-level abstractions. Then when we say "democracy means many things," we probably won't have to make clear whether we mean (a) "The word 'democracy' is used in many ways," (b) "Democracy (I mean a form of government—I'm not sure exactly what form) causes different people to react in different ways," or maybe something else. The desire to make profound-sounding utterances without being asked for clarifications has done much to inhibit the development of a precise meta-language.

The use of quotation marks. Perhaps the most consistent meta-linguistic system in use is that of quotation marks. The convention is this: **When a linguistic formulation is enclosed in quotation marks, reference is being made to the language so enclosed. All formulations not so enclosed refer to something outside themselves.** Worded another way, language **talked about** shall be enclosed in quotes; language **used** shall not be so enclosed. For example:

> Sky is blue. (I'm talking about that stuff over our heads.)
>
> "Sky" has three letters. (I'm talking about a word.)

This would seem to be a clear and simple distinction, enabling one to speak alternately of a thing and its name by non-use or use of quotation marks. But aside from the fact that quotation marks can't be produced orally, other traditional and habitual uses of quotes have clouded the issue. Here are examples of such current uses:

1. He's one of those "liberals." (Meaning: He calls himself "liberal," but the word "liberal" has no business referring to what he really is.)
2. Some authors try to separate "body" and "soul." (Meaning [I think]: The entities to which some authors refer when they say "body" and "soul" do not in fact exist separately.)
3. All phenomena are intricately related in "The Greater Cosmos." (Meaning: Watch out for that phrase in quotes—I have only the vaguest idea what I want to mean by it!)
4. Freshman students are requested to engage in a "minimum" of extracurricular activities. (Meaning: You will have to use your own judgment as to how much activity comprises a minimum.)
5. Freshman students are requested to participate in a minimum of "extracurricular" activities. (Meaning: I am using the word "extracurricular" in an unusual way. With this hint you should be able to figure what I do mean.)

These five illustrations represent only a fraction of the current uses of quotation marks. Many of these uses are codified into a system of sorts and may in certain contexts be quite useful.[4] Presumably a single, consistent use of quotation marks will best facilitate the extensive study of language contemplated here. Therefore, quotation marks will be used hereafter in accordance with the convention italicized earlier—as a reference to symbols, not to things symbolized—and in no other way. But be warned: Because of the wide variety of

[4] Irving Lee, "General Semantics: 1952," **Etc.**, IX, No. 2 (1952), 103 and *passim*.

traditional and current usage, strict adherence to such a convention will not be easy. Other writers, unimpressed by the agreement you and I have just made, will of course continue to use quotation marks as they have in the past. You may on occasion find yourself rewriting the discourse of others to shake the persistent and varied uses of quotation marks therein. But mostly you need guard against your own tendency to use quotes as a substitute for linguistic precision.

One exception to the general rule should be noted: In journalistic reporting it is often necessary to mark the point at which the speaker's exact words are being used. A reporter may begin the sentence by paraphrasing his subject and end with his last few words in quotation marks, indicating that at this point he has ceased using his own words and begun a direct quote. In a sense this practice fits our convention, as the quotation marks say in effect "he used these words."

At this point, armed with a way to talk about language, we are ready to look at meaning as a property of language—that is, to discover **how language means**—and then to observe the many ways in which units of language can be meaningful.

Summary

A language is an organized set of symbols with rules of syntax. To be useful a language must be definite, consistent and universal among its users. To talk about language a meta-language is needed. Ours will be a single, consistent use of quotation marks to enclose that portion of language to be discussed.

Questions and exercises

1. Which of the following are linguistic symbols?

    the   cat   pfft!   xlpoz   only   ?   卐

2. Assuming all quotation marks to have been used **according to our convention,** label each of the following "true," "false," "indeterminate" (either true or false), or "nonsense":

"x" is a number	sky has three letters	Tom is a name
"sky is "blue"	"sky" has three letters	"Tom" is a name
"sky" is sky	"blue" is "blue"	"blue" is blue

3. Find a recording of Victor Borge's "Phonetic Punctuation" and listen to it carefully. Is he using quotation marks according to our agreement? Would phonetic punctuation aid aural comprehension?

TWO

How language means

If a person of questionable integrity were to step up to you and accuse you of being "the most deliberate blathersnicker he had ever known," you might call him a liar on general principles. Even those of you who were alert enough to say to yourselves, "I don't know what 'blather-snicker' means," may admit to a tiny bit of resentment at being so categorized. As we noted in the introduction, there is an almost irresistible urge to predicate truth before meaning has been ascertained. Part of the reason for this reluctance to pause over meaning lies in its seeming simplicity. Meaning **ought** to be an easy problem. All we have to do is define our terms.

If meaning were that simple one would not need to study semantics. But the problems of meaning in language are so formidable that centuries of efforts by skilled linguists have barely touched them. In addition to the many real problems in this area, false and needless snags have arisen on the basis that "meaning" had some exact discernible signification. The word "meaning" may of course mean whatever its users want it to mean. To agree on a usage for this book, let's eliminate some obviously extraneous concepts.

What we don't mean by "meaning"

The word "meaning" (or "mean" or "means" or "meaningful" or any of the other cognates) crops up in some strange linguistic neighborhoods. Here are two examples:

The professor is a mean old man.
I mean to go downtown tomorrow.

In the first example "mean" is an adjective meaning "unkind" or "vicious" or "vindictive" or something of the sort. As far as we know this word "mean" has no connection with the "mean" that we are trying to focus on. In the second example "mean" is a colloquial substitute for "intend"—again, no connection with meaning in our sense.

Here are some other uses a bit more akin to our interests but still not quite what we want:

White means purity.
This locket means a great deal to me.
He is scratching on the door; that means he wants to go out.
A red sunset means warm weather is coming.
He gave her a meaning (meaningful) look.

The first two examples are cases of non-linguistic symbolism. White as a color (not the word "white") is declared to symbolize purity for a using community. The locket is said to contain symbolic significance for the author, who in this case comprises the entire using community. In either case no language is involved. The third and fourth sentences exemplify not **meaning** but **inference.** The sunset does not mean the warm weather; its presence is used as a basis for **inferring** the imminence of warm weather. The door-scratching situation admittedly leaves room for argument; that is, it may be argued that the dog (if that is what "he" refers to) is actually communicating his desires to us.[1] Most experts insist, however, that animals have yet to develop a verifiable language for communicating with humans. Again, in the last example one might maintain that there is a special language of glances. But our definition of "language" requires a set of syntactical rules. And one would be hard put to codify the syntax of an arched eyebrow or an over-the-shoulder grin.

The meaning-relation in language (linguistic meaning)

If the above do not exemplify linguistic meaning—what does? First, we should observe that four items are usually present when language is used meaningfully:

[1] Roger Brown, **Words and Things** (Glencoe, Ill.: The Free Press, 1958), pp. 3–10.

A piece of language
A producer (speaker or writer)
One or more consumers (listeners or readers)
A piece of the world outside the language to which the producer presumably wishes to refer his consumers.

When these factors are present, and certain symbolic agreement exists between the producer and consumer, linguistic meaning occurs. Indeed the relation described among these four items **is** meaning; and it is to this fourfold relation that we shall be referring when we use the word "meaning" and its cognates.

Recent widespread development in communication theory has resulted in a rash of models that purport to illustrate the process by which meaning is transferred linguistically from one person to another.[2] While such models may on occasion be oversimplified and therefore misleading, the following triangular model is offered as a graphic equivalent of the fourfold definition given above.

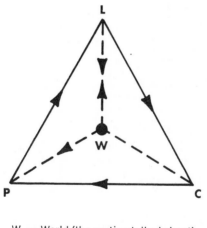

W = World (the portion talked about)
P = Producer
L = Language (Symbol)
C = Consumer

---

[2] E.g., Claude E. Shannon and Warren Weaver, **The Mathematical Theory of Communication** (Urbana, Ill.: The University of Illinois Press, 1964).

Note that the meaning-process starts not with language itself but with a portion of the world. The producer writes or utters a portion of the language which for him is tied symbolically to this piece of the world he wishes to refer to. (This part of the process is sometimes called "encoding.") The language reaches the consumer, who is able by experience or prior agreement to focus on that same portion of the world (decoding). The consumer—by action, by subliminal nuance, or by the production of language of his own (feedback) gives indication that the linguistic connection has been made.

The ways in which language can be meaningful

It may be tempting to assume from the foregoing treatment of "meaning" that a given piece of language is either meaningful or not meaningful, and that is the end of the matter. Clearly this is not the case. Aside from the shades of meanings and degrees of meaningfulness, we see immediately that not all language is used in the same way; that there are various **kinds** of linguistic meaning. Let's begin by looking at some samples:

1. The British Government, which watches closely the racial moods and civil-rights legislation in the United States, is taking strong measures to curb race discrimination at home.

    A new race bill, expected to be published around Easter, will deal with discrimination in public and private housing, employment, education, insurance, and credit.

    Colored immigrants long have resented the fact that they often have to pay substantially higher rates for car insurance, mortgages, and installment buying than established citizens.

    Under the proposed legislation, penalties for such charges may be as high as $1,200.[3]

2. Our great Ship is foundering on the foam of indecision. There is nobody at the wheel. Our Captain is a mere ghost, going through the motions of leadership. Meanwhile the rocks of fascism loom on the right, while the deceptive whirlpools of socialism and communism draw our ship inexorably to the left. Unless a strong, firm hand takes the wheel—now—and steers a firm course through these troubled waters, the Ship men thought unsinkable will go down to oblivion.[4]

[3] **Christian Science Monitor** (Boston), April 6–8, 1968, p. 2.
[4] This passage and all others not specifically documented should be credited to the author.

3. He who enters the sphere of faith enters the sanctuary of life. Where there is faith there is an awareness of holiness. . . . What concerns one ultimately becomes holy. The awareness of the holy is awareness of the presence of the divine, namely of the content of our ultimate concern. . . . It is a presence which remains mysterious in spite of its appearance, and it exercises both an attractive and a repulsive function on those who encounter it. . . . The reason for these two effects of the holy is obvious if we see the relation of the experience of the holy to the experience of ultimate concern. The human heart seeks the infinite because that is where the finite wants to rest. In the infinite it sees its own fulfillment. This is the reason for the ecstatic attraction and fascination of everything in which ultimacy is manifest. On the other hand, if ultimacy is manifest and exercises its fascinating attraction, one realizes at the same time the infinite distance of the finite from the infinite and, consequently, the negative judgment over any finite attempts to reach the infinite. The feeling of being consumed in the presence of the divine is a profound expression of man's relation to the holy. It is implied in every genuine act of faith, in every state of ultimate concern.[5]

4. When more and more children leave school, the enrollment goes down.

   If two straight lines cannot enclose an area, then the sum of the angles in a triangle cannot be greater than 180°.

   Business is business.

Having read these passages you should sense at least a vague difference among them. The difference lies not in subject matter, nor to any notable extent in the language used, but rather in the way in which the authors go about their descriptions. To delineate these differences a little more finely we must examine each passage individually.

The first passage seems to require no special kind of interpretation. Its treatment of racial discrimination is forthright and direct. The things, people, and transaction the passage talks about are readily found in the world. Some of the words used may require definitions; but the general approach to the communication task we shall call **referential** (literal, descriptive)[6] meaning.

At first glance the second passage would seem to be talking about

---

[5] Paul Tillich, **Dynamics of Faith** (New York: Harper & Row, 1957; London: George Allen & Unwin Ltd.), pp. 12–13. Reprinted by permission of the publishers.
[6] These words are used synonymously in this context.

ships and water and rocks and whirlpools. But even without the context, the presence of such words as "fascism," "socialism," and "communism" tells us the passage is not about navigation but about something else. If we were to go out into the world and look for the
rocks and whirlpools talked about, we would not find them. When a
passage of this sort makes claims which are literally unlikely or absurd—as this one does—we should assume that the meaning intended
is not literal but rather **metaphorical** (figurative).[7]

As we look through the passage on "Faith" and attempt to tie the
words it uses to the things of the world, we find once again that we
cannot. But the reason here is not the same as with the ship of state.
In that passage the things talked about were concrete enough—they
simply were not there. Here the author uses words we are familiar with;
but he puts them together in a strange way; such that the end effect
seems to reach beyond the sensible world. At first we are tempted to
toss it off under the label of "high-level abstraction," which it as-
suredly is. But the concept of discrimination encountered in the first
passage is surely an abstraction as well. The difference is that the
author of the "Faith" passage, while he presumably expects his discourse to influence the activities of the physical world, would never
expect this passage to be reducible to any literal equivalent. Language
used in this way is said to exhibit **metaphysical** meaning.

The communicator of metaphysics has a challenging task: to describe the spiritual world in a largely sense-oriented language. When
I say "the sky is blue," how do you know whether I have told the
truth or not? Simply by going out and looking. But when I say "God is
love," where do you go, to what do you look for verification? As noted
above, such statements refer not to things we can look at, hear, smell,
feel or taste, but to something else. Yet most of our language was built
to deal with the material world—with things, people, and the sometimes complicated transactions among them. Purely metaphysical assertion purports to talk about something separate from the material
world; something which may influence its activities but is not reducible to its components. Thus we regard metaphysical meaning as a
separate function of language. The same four elements are there: a
producer, a consumer, some language and the thing referred to—but

---

[7] Although metaphors are only one class of figurative language, the other kinds
occur so seldom with referential intent that we use the two words (figurative and
metaphorical) synonymously.

the method of transportation is not the same. The way in which sense-oriented words are related to the spiritual world is in some way different from the standard encoding and decoding process. Without attempting here to investigate the precise nature of this phenomenon, let us agree to treat metaphysical language as a thing apart.

The sentences listed under (4) may seem at first glance to have no connection one with another. Each seems understandable enough; and certainly none of us would wish to challenge the truth of any. They would seem then to be unrelated assertions, meaningful in the same (referential) way as the statements in the racial discrimination passage—except for one factor: **None of these three sentences is capable of being false.** After careful definitions are applied the first may be rewritten "when more and more children leave school, more and more children leave school." Or "when the enrollment goes down, the enrollment goes down"—both automatically true. The second statement is an automatic consequence of Euclidean geometry. Given the proper premise, its truth cannot be questioned. "Business is business," assuming that "business" does not slip a cog in the course of the sentence, must surely be true.

The truth of statements such as these follows immediately from their formulation. To understand them is to believe them. This automatic truth property, as we shall see later, has an important bearing on the way in which they mean. Language used in such a way is called **tautology** or said to have **tautological** meaning.

We have considered four ways in which language can be meaningful: referentially, metaphorically, metaphysically and tautologically. Presumably there are others.[8] And now, having made the distinction, one wonders if it was worth the effort. Surely the "Ship of State" passage, if one takes it at all, would never be taken as literal discourse. Pure metaphysics we are not likely to mix up with other forms. And tautologies—at least in the naked form in which they appear above—should

[8] P. W. Bridgeman argues for a fifth kind of meaning as follows: "What, for instance, is the meaning of the statement that the distance between the planes of atoms in a certain crystal is 3×10^8 cm.? What we would like to mean is that $1/3 \times 10^8$ of these planes piled on top of each other gives a thickness of 1 cm; but of course such a meaning is not the actual one. The actual meaning may be found by examining the operations by which we arrive at the number 3×10^8. As a matter of fact, 3×10^8 was the number obtained by solving a general equation derived from the wave theory of light, into which certain numerical data obtained by experiments with x-rays have been substituted. Thus has the character of the concept of length changed from tactual to optical."

be easy to spot and not likely to cause trouble. So why make the distinction in the first place?

The reason is that most speakers and writers like to mix many kinds of meaning into one piece of discourse. Furthermore, what looks like one kind of meaning often turns out to hide another. Take another look at the "Get Tough" passage at the beginning of Chapter One. If you look closely you can find examples of all four meanings, often deeply intertwined one with another. But much more important, the **meaning form** in which much of the discourse appears may belie the **meaning function** the author obviously intended. To understand how this can happen let's look at an example of pure figurative writing:

> And a thousand thousand slimy things
> Lived on; and so did I.[9]

These lines from Coleridge's "Ancient Mariner" exhibit figurative meaning. This places them in the same category with the "Ship of State" passage. The important difference—aside from a minor degree of literary quality—is that the Coleridge poem makes no claim to literal description of the real world. There is no point whatever in asking whether the author actually counted the slimy things, or in demanding an explanation of "slimy." The poem is successful or unsuccessful completely apart from these matters. The "Ship of State" passage, on the other hand, to the extent that it is capable of making any sense at all, becomes meaningful only when we sort out the metaphors, replacing ships, captains, rocks and whirlpools with their literal equivalents. Thus, while we are happy to leave the Coleridge poem alone, rejoicing in its creativity, we remain alert to those metaphors which may hide important referential intent.

The picture is further complicated when metaphors are thrust into the midst of otherwise referential discourse. You should have seen quite a bit of these in the "Get Tough" passage. And the referential discourse on racial discrimination takes on a new tone when we add a paragraph that was cut from the original:

> The new bill comes at a time when the government has been badly
> stung by criticism from the National Committee for Commonwealth
> Immigrants. The committee accuses the government of steamrolling

[9] Samuel Taylor Coleridge, **The Rime of the Ancient Mariner,** Part IV.

through Parliament discriminatory legislation which restricts the entry of Kenyan Asians holding British passports.[10]

If we had to classify this paragraph as to the way in which it is meaningful we would have to say "referential." But the words "stung" and "steamrolling" bear the unmistakable mark of metaphor. Knowing as we do that the author did not mean these words literally, we remain alert to the need to replace them with what he did mean. And this involves a bit of guessing.

What about Tillich's metaphysical passage on Faith? Is there an important referential equivalent here? While a handful of modern metaphysicians insist that their doctrines can meet the tests of logic and semantics and thus can be said in alternative language, most of them quite properly object to any attempt to translate their writings into referential discourse. Their assertions are written as they are because of the nature of their subject matter. There is no referential equivalent; and to attempt to render these eternal truths in less than spiritual language is to dilute them and destroy their efficacy. If the consumer of metaphysical discourse does not understand what he reads or hears, restating in material language will not help him. He must rather study and restudy the original metaphysical statements, and through prayer and divine revelation he will come to understand. In this book we accept the latter position; and no attempts will be made to rewrite metaphysics.

But what about those tautologies? When one says "Business is business," is one only parroting the obvious; or is one perhaps implying a few of one's pet ideas as to how business should operate? Such a tautological statement (and its half-brother, the self-contradiction— "Business is not business"—which must always be false) may look like a part of everyday discourse. Indeed the tautology seems especially valuable because its truth cannot be questioned. But as with fool's gold its glitter must be eschewed. For with all its truth it tells nothing of the world we want to know about. Business is indeed business; but this tells us nothing about how business is or should be conducted. Business would be business even if there were no business—just so "business" has the same meaning at both ends of the sentence. If on the other hand when I utter the bland assertion "Business is business" I mean that certain inhuman practices that would be unthinkable in

[10] **Christian Science Monitor,** op. cit.

any other social context are quite permissible in the business world, I have indeed made an important referential assertion. But even as my utterance takes on the color of referential significance it loses the safe must-be-true quality of the tautology; it may well be false.

What have we said here? Simply that discourse which **seems** to be meaningful in some non-referential way (particularly metaphorical and tautological language) may in fact hide an important referential equivalent which is the writer's or speaker's real intent. Furthermore, modern discourse—produced by us or somebody else—doesn't end up in neat packages labeled "referential," "metaphorical," etc. It rather hits us in jumbles: questions, commands, metaphors, tautologies, linguistic meanings of all kinds may be found in a single paragraph. If we wish to extract from any communication those portions which really intend to make claims about this world—that is, with referential intent—some kind of translation is in order. But in trying to fix the precise form we would like our discourse to end up in, it becomes necessary to understand the various kinds of **sentences** in which referential language may appear. And as this will require an entire chapter we must defer detailed consideration of translation until that chapter has been assimilated.

Summary

The word "meaning" can itself have many meanings. For our use it will refer to that fourfold relationship among a producer of discourse, the consumer, the discourse itself, and the thing referred to. Language itself may be meaningful in many ways. Four of these are: referential, metaphorical, metaphysical and tautological. When non-referential language clothes a referential intent, better understanding can often be achieved by rewriting in referential language.

Questions and exercises

1. Would it be possible for linguistic meaning to take place if **one** of the **four criteria** were missing? What happens to the process if the thing referred to doesn't exist?
2. Check your morning newspaper for editorials or advertisements containing non-referential language. What change would be effected on these communications if the non-referential portions were rewritten in referential language? Would this be possible in every case?

3. Go over the "Get Tough" selection in Chapter One in the same way, underlining the non-referential portions. (Don't be misled into underlining everything with **meaning** problems—that comes later.) Does your underlining necessarily indicate **criticism** of those portions of the passage?

4. Label each of the following sentences regarding the **kind of meaning** it exemplifies.

   a. Holy smoke!
   b. Whom do you think you are pushing?
   c. We are in the hands of the Almighty.
   d. An "F" is an "F".
   e. While the hawks and the doves squabble over Viet Nam, the chickens dodge the draft.

Now reread the instructions for this question and count your answers. (If you have more than four, you missed the boat!) Of the sentences you labeled other than "referential," which, if any, do you believe has referential intent? Are you sure?

THREE

How sentences mean

"Say, did you get an eyeful of that new . . ."

"Did I ever! In the library, you mean. He was leaning against the . . ."

"Right! That's the one. Boy he sure is . . ."

"You know it! I wonder if he's . . ."

"I don't think so because when he took off his gloves I got a look at . . ."

"Yes, but that doesn't mean anything. I mean as good-looking as he is and all . . ."

"Yeah, I guess you're right. Let's forget about it. Which reminds me, what about that . . ."

"Now you're talking!"

Surely you have heard a conversation recently which resembled the above. If you had heard this one instead of reading it you might have been tempted to say, "What is so unusual about that?" But those ominous dots at the end of each line must have called your attention to the fact that, until the end, nobody completed a sentence. The remarkable fact is that **communication took place**—successful communication, if past experience is any guide.

Exercise: Give a large group of people copies of the above conversation and ask them to complete (on paper working independently) each unfinished sentence as they think it would have ended had the speaker been permitted to finish. After eliminating the obvious attempts to be funny, you should find a remarkable agreement among the participants. A second and even more remarkable fact is that we should expect people to talk in sentences in the first place. What is this preoccupation with the sentence that leads teachers of English to screech with red pencils at every fragment? What is a sentence in the first place?

The nature of the sentence

Somewhere way back in school you were probably told that a sentence is a unit of language that expresses a complete thought. Unless you were the kind of person who automatically accepts everything he learns in school, you probably felt a bit uncomfortable about that definition. Perhaps you even raised some verbal objection. For surely in the proper context "ouch!" expresses as complete a thought as any sentence. And yet most grammarians would reject this single ejaculation as a candidate for sentenceship. The fact is that we define "sentence" in one way and think of it in another. And no matter how we switch the definition around it never seems quite to describe the category we want to circumscribe. It seems a sentence is one of those things we all recognize but nobody can define.

Assuming for a moment that you and I know a sentence when we see one, why should we care? We care because we desire truth. We want to separate truth from falsity because this will help us to control our environment. And when we look to language for truth (or for falsity) we find it comes to us in sentences. A word cannot be true. A paragraph is true in a special sense only when its component sentences are true. Thus, our momentary preoccupation as semanticists with the sentence: If we can ever get one in shape so it can be understood, perhaps we (or someone else) can examine it for truth. With this in mind it will pay us to consider the various **forms** in which legitimate sentences may appear, so that we can start setting up some criteria for their meaningfulness.

Traditional (formal) classification of sentences.   Grammarians traditionally classify sentences as follows:

Declarative:	John went home.
Interrogative:	Did John go home?
Imperative:	John, go home.
Exclamatory:	I wish John would go home!

If we examine these forms carefully we see that the exclamation is not really a special class of sentence. Exclamations are either complete sentences, as exemplified above, or fragments (e.g., "Holy smoke!"). If they are complete sentences, they will always fall into one of the three other types (declarative, interrogative, or imperative). Thus it would be possible in theory to eliminate the exclamatory sentence as a class. But further investigation shows that the **expressive function** is an important one in language, and deserves separation from other functions. This leads us to a reclassification of sentences in terms of how they work rather than what they look like.

Functional classification of sentences. Many different sentential functions may be observed in everyday language. It might even be asserted that every sentence we utter has a slightly different purpose. Classical trends lead us to note three general functions, as follows:

Cognitive (informative):	to convey information
Directive:	to influence conduct
Expressive:	to express (or evoke) emotion

As with the sentential forms listed earlier, these functions purport to be exhaustive; that is, to cover all the functions a sentence can have. In practice of course, the three-fold classification must on occasion break down. Many sentences may function in two or three ways at the same time. To locate the precise function of a given sentence may require deep analysis, analysis which extends beyond the sentence itself into the inner motives of its producer. This kind of spotlight we would be reluctant to shine on our own discourse, let alone someone else's. One must also contend with the argument that **any** sentence aimed at an audience functions largely as a changer of actions or attitudes; that its producer would ultimately accept only such change as a sign of communication success or failure. Nevertheless, the **immediate** function of most sentences is readily discernible and, as we shall see, sometimes remarkably different than its form would suggest.

Form versus function. If we are going to classify sentences by their **function** rather than the more familiar **form,** then our first job is to chart some kind of equivalence so we can tell what goes with what:

FORM	FUNCTION
Declarative sentence	Cognitive
Imperative	Directive
Exclamatory fragment	Expressive
Interrogative sentence	?

What happens to the interrogative form? Declarative sentences are presumably cognitive in function. Imperatives (commands) are directive and exclamations are expressive. But what about questions?

One view asserts that the question functions as a kind of directive because it seeks to evoke a special (verbal) kind of conduct. Another argument calls it a kind of cognitive; one that seeks information rather than providing it. Our inability to settle this matter immediately seems to suggest that we don't know as much about questions as we need to.

Questions: theory and types. As a linguistic device the question seems simple enough: One asks a question because one wants information. In a moment we shall see some other reasons for asking questions. But first we must direct our attention to the astonishing fact that as a tool of the English language the question is totally and completely expendable. We don't need it. If you doubt this, invent a situation that calls for a question, and in place of the question put a command. For example:

> What time is it? (Imperative equivalent: Please tell me the time.) Are you going to church tomorrow? (Imperative equivalent: Tell me whether you are going to church tomorrow.)

The same substitution can be made for any question which genuinely seeks information. Granted, the listener (who may be accustomed to more customary and polite verbal forms) may respond rather coolly to your demand for information. But this is a colloquial fetish which we would soon get over. Besides, we all know questions which, no matter how prettily we ask them, won't be answered. This discovery—that any genuine question can be replaced by a command—seems to argue for the notion that questions are after all directive in function. But before committing ourselves, let's examine some **types** of questions.

Of the two questions exemplified above, the second seems more difficult to replace by a command; that is, the replacement is more awkward. In fact, grammatically these questions show little resemblance one to the other. Actually they illustrate an important distinction between two types of questions: the open-end (interrogative) question and the yes-or-no (poll-type) questions. That is, questions beginning with an auxiliary (helping) verb are (with one small exception to be noted directly) answerable by yes or no. Questions beginning with interrogative pronouns or adjectives ("who," "what," "when," "where," and the like) are not.

With this distinction in mind, and looking at the examples above, it would seem that yes-or-no questions function more as cognitives while open-end questions seem more like directives. But the matter is too complex to settle so easily.

> Is it later than we think?
> What are we waiting for?

With great care and effort we might be able to devise a situation where the first example could actually be requesting information. That is, the asker really wants to know if it is later by the clock than we (whomever that may include) think. Much more likely is that notion that he wants, not an answer, but rather to convey information ("it is later than we think.") or perhaps to secure action ("let's do something about it!"). For the second example we would need to look at the context before we could say whether the asker wanted information; but most likely his seeming question is a call to action. A question that functions in this way is called a **rhetorical question.**

How are we to know whether a question is real or rhetorical? In oral communication the tone of voice usually tells us. In writing one must rely on context; if the sentences following the question seem to provide an answer then the question was rhetorical, not real. In fact it may be stated as a general rule that in written discourse which is mass communicated (via magazines, newspapers, etc.) questions are likely to be rhetorical rather than real. The reason for this assumption is obvious. A real question calls for an answer; and the writer is separated from his readers (except in the "please write in" situation) so that an actual answer is impossible. In any case the rhetorical question which hides an assertion should be carefully watched for: it will probably require translation.

Another question not to be answered is the **reiterative question.**

> You don't like this subject, do you.

This so-called question is really a statement, isn't it. We call it a question because of the "do you" at the end. But all it asks for is confirmation of what is said in the first place. It tries to browbeat you into the right answer. So self-assertive is the reiterative question that in most courts of law one is permitted to use it only on hostile witnesses.

Still another type of question requires our attention: the **alternative question.**

Will you have soup or salad?
Shall we turn left, right, or go straight ahead?

This is the exception you were warned about earlier: a question that starts with a helping verb but still is not in its intended sense answerable by yes or no. When the asker says "soup or salad?" he obviously expects you to pick one of the two. Whether you should be bound by the alternative offered is a contextual matter; that is, in the soup-or-salad case you may wish to respond "neither" or, hopefully, "both." Of course the alternative question is technically answerable by yes or no. If you said "yes" to the soup question you would presumably be satisfied with either choice.[1] When I was learning to play golf every ball I hit would curl out of sight, first to the left and then to the right. Unsure of golfing terminology I asked my patient and experienced partner, "What's my trouble, do I slice or hook?" to which he replied safely, "Yes!"

After probing rather deeply into the nature of the question we still don't know whether its function is cognitive or directive. We did decide that yes-or-no questions seem more cognitive while open-end questions act more like directives. The rhetorical question by its very nature is more likely to be directive than cognitive. The reiterative question is clearly a thinly disguised cognitive with a polite "do you?" curling up from the end like a pig's tail. The alternative question, being a hybrid, could go either way. It seems in the end we must allow for both functions, which means rewriting our form-function chart as follows:

We have had enough trouble getting this chart in shape; but as it was with the classification of linguistic meaning—a metaphorical or tautological **form** often hiding a referential **function**—so it is with sentences. The chart assumes a **normal** correlation between sentential form and function. That is, if one utters a declarative sentence one

---

[1] Logicians call this process "affirming the weak disjunction"—that is, declaring either **or both** of two alternatives to be true or acceptable.

normally expects it to be cognitive in function. But as we saw in our study of questions, the form of the sentence is no guarantee as to its function. Let's look at some examples:

> Trespassers will be prosecuted.

This is a declarative sentence and we would normally expect a cognitive function; that is, we would expect the author's intent to be the conveying of some kind of information. But as we examine the sentence in its anticipated context—on a gate or in front of a lawn—we become immediately suspicious of the cognitive intent. Surely the author is less interested in informing passersby of the laws of private property than in getting them to stay off a given piece of land. Schematically, form-function disparity looks like this:

> Trespassers will be prosecuted   Form: Declarative
>
> (Meaning)
> Keep off the grass!   Function: Directive

And to list further examples:

> Insert (your) pencil here.   Form: Imperative
>
> (Meaning)
> If you insert your pencil here
> you will automatically sharpen it.   Function: Cognitive
>
> (She to him during midnight stroll)
> Oh what a beautiful moon!   Form: Exclamatory fragment
>
> (Meaning)
> ?   Function: ?

Translation

We have now looked at two ways producers of discourse may say one thing and mean another. In Chapter Two we were concerned with language that was non-referential in form but which hid a referential intent. In this chapter we uncovered a similar disparity between form and function—with particular concern for the non-declarative sentence which clothes a cognitive intent. How are we to react to such language? Some kind of translation is clearly in order. But before undertaking such an adventure we had best know what we are about.

It is important at the outset that we steel ourselves against any sense of condemnation of the discourse we propose to rewrite. We have no sure way of knowing on what level the speaker or writer wants to communicate. Maybe that high-flown extended metaphor was a deliberate attempt to be literary, with little or no referential intent involved. And maybe that question was not rhetorical at all, but a genuine attempt to secure information. In short, the assumption of cognitive intent is a big one, and should not be made lightly.

If, however, we do assume a referential, cognitive intent, are we still not taking a lot on ourselves to rewrite somebody's communication? After all, whoever put this discourse together probably went to considerable effort to impart style and verve to his linguistic effort. By what authority do we recommit it to laborious, pedestrian, literal prose? Clearly there is no thought to correct or improve, but rather to understand. If the author's intent is indeed literal—if there is some basic attempt to make a claim about the world—then this claim deserves to be understood. And our best chance to understand it is to put it into the form in which such claims are normally made, namely, the referential statement. For example:

We are discussing the difficulty of identifying Communists in the United States, and someone says, "Well, all I can say is that if something looks like a duck, walks like a duck, and quacks like a duck, it's a duck!" The hasty analyst might dismiss the remark as irrelevant, since the habits of ducks are not at issue. Such dismissal could be grossly unfair to the speaker, who quite clearly is not talking about ducks but about something else. If the remark is to be taken seriously it must be translated into referential language, perhaps as follows:

> Persons exhibiting certain characteristics (to be listed later) are (probably?) Communists.
>
> **OR**
>
> A Communist can be identified by his general pattern of words and deeds.

In the above example the entire sentence comprised a metaphor. Such figures are usually quite easy to spot, though not always easy to translate. But speakers and writers are quick to pop single-word metaphors unexpectedly into otherwise literal discourse. When someone speaks of taking a hand in a game of tennis, you are not likely to class such language as metaphorical, even though you are aware that "taking a hand" is not meant literally. In any case, it isn't very important whether we call this communication metaphorical or not, since we all understand what was intended. But when someone characterizes militant student demonstrations as "changing the entire face of the campus," we may not be quite so sure. We know that "face" is not meant literally—but how is it meant? In the final analysis we are going to have to rewrite "face" in its literal equivalent—as nearly as we can guess what it is—before we can say we really understand what is being asserted.

Sentential translation. As we have seen throughout this chapter finding (or rendering) discourse in referential form won't always see us home. Many kinds of sentences—notably rhetorical questions—turn up in contents which inform us that their authors are trying to tell us something. When this happens it is once again our duty to rewrite the claim in a declarative (referential) form. Let's look again at an example from a few pages back.

Is it later than we think?

As we already noted the asker really doesn't want to know anything. But **what** he is telling us is another matter. The obvious translation would be "It is later than we think"; but taken literally this assertion borders on the absurd. How does the author know how late we think it is? Clearly he means to say more than this, perhaps something like "If we fail to act now, we may find our objectives unattainable."

How do we know whether the asker wants a yes or a no answer? That is, why couldn't we translate the original question: "It is **not** later than we think"? Of course the context in which the question was asked will normally tell us whether an affirmative or negative equivalent is intended. As an additional guide we may follow the general rule that questions asked **affirmatively** imply a **negative** assertion and vice-versa.[2]

Are we going to put up with this?

(Translation)
We are not going (ought not) to put up with this.

Isn't it obvious what he's after?

(Translation)
It's obvious what he's after.

[2] John Hughes, **The Science of Language: An Introduction to Linguistics** (New York: Random House, 1962), p. 178.

It may be easier as we study a given piece of discourse to tell **when** translation is needed than to see exactly **how** to go about it. These three steps should help you to get into referential form those passages which are cognitive in intent:

1. Search the context for cognitive intent.
2. Change the language only to the degree required to achieve referential form.
3. Say no more or less than the original justifies.

Applications

For the public speaker.   For those seeking to improve their speech composition there may seem little point in rewriting everything in referential statement form. Probably some of you have gone to considerable pains to lift your discourse out of the humdrum, and are not about to drag it back to insipid literal form. And in this bent you are eminently sound. But it will still pay you to know when you are speaking figuratively and when literally. You can profit from distinguishing rhetorical questions which you may use as introductions and transitions, from those which are actually substitutes for what you had to say. How many of the latter did you have in the last speech you delivered? Can you restate each one in referential form? If not, your preparation process—that rigorous private thinking which must precede public speaking—may need careful reexamination.

For the debater.   Argumentative speakers—particularly those subject to cross-examination—will want to make careful note of the kinds of questions distinguished in this chapter. As already noted one can tell at the beginning of a question whether it will be answerable by yes or no, or whether it will require for an answer some kind of statement. This is particularly important when one is subjected to unfair yes-or-no questions. (The classic example, "Have you stopped beating your wife?" is a prototype.) The fact that a question **can** be answered yes-or-no does not mean that it should be so answered. Likewise, one needs to be alert to the reiterative question, which tends to put words in one's mouth. And finally there is the alternative question, which seeks conveniently to eliminate the possibility of a third or fourth choice.

For the bi-lingual student.   The structure and function of English sentences may often serve as a clue for pronouncing them. You may on occasion have puzzled over the advice, "Always raise your voice at the end of a question," particularly when you found that such practice was right only about half the time! In general, yes-or-no questions take a rising inflection; open-end (interrogative) questions call for a falling intonation. In alternative questions, the voice rises with every alternative except the last, on which it falls. The reiterative question is spoken like what it really is in function: a statement.

Summary

Sentences come to us in three forms—not in four, as traditional grammar insists. These three forms—declarative, interrogative, and imperative—correspond to the classical functions of discourse (cognitive, directive, and expressive), though not in a one-to-one correlation. The **form** in which a sentence may appear is not a necessary indication of the **function** which may be intended. Whenever the intent is obviously cognitive, even though the form may be otherwise, better understanding may be achieved through translation to referential statement form. It is these statements and only these that are capable of truth or falsity.

Questions and exercises

1. See how many different examples you can construct illustrating form-function disparity in sentences. For example, can you invent a situation which would produce a sentence **interrogative** in form but **expressive** in function?
2. Assuming a cognitive function in each of the following, translate to referential statements:
   a. Why do today what you can put off 'til tomorrow?
   b. Carry me back to Old Virginny.
3. Find the questions and commands (if any) in the "Get Tough" passage at the beginning of Chapter One. Are any of these cognitive in function? If so, translate to referential statement(s).
4. Dust off one of your old speeches and see how many examples you can find of:
   a. non-referential language which is referential in intent.
   b. questions or commands which are cognitive in intent.

   Do these form-function disparities add to or detract from the quality of your speech? Why?

FOUR

How words mean

The next time it rains and you have nothing to do, copy a sentence of considerable length—perhaps the sentence you are now reading— onto a piece of paper. Next, cut the sentence up into separate words and drop the words into a hat. Then pull the words one by one out of the hat and place them on a desk in the order in which they were drawn. Unless you're incredibly lucky, the string of words in front of you will be complete gibberish.

The point of this exercise is that it takes more than meaningful words to make a meaningful sentence. Those words in the hat were meaningful in their original form; but somehow their capacity to make sense together disappeared when the order was changed. And although no one in his right mind would put words together in such a random fashion, it is plain that the order in which English words can make sense is subject to certain rules. This collection of rules is called **syntax.** And while it might seem more sensible to find out first how words mean, and second how they go together, we're going to reverse this process for reasons which will become clear later on.

Syntactical meaning

Perhaps the best way to introduce the concept of syntax is to relate it to a more familiar notion called "grammar." These two terms are often used interchangeably. But we shall need to make a rough distinction as follows: Grammar concerns itself with language rules of all kinds, including verb inflection, plurals, and other requirements which may be purely conventional or arbitrary. Syntax is limited to those positional factors in language which affect meaning. Thus "We was there" is a violation of the rules of grammar; it is perfectly easily understood even though we know it is wrong. "The man tall" (as a substitute for "the tall man") is a violation of syntax. Thus, the syntax of a language may be said to be the set of rules and principles which governs the ways in which its component parts may go together and make sense.

It may be argued that a study of such rules, while interesting to the linguist, is of little value to seekers after meaning. After all, people don't go around pulling words out of hats, nor do normal speakers of English utter phrases like "the man tall." True in varying degree, but there are at least two important reasons why lay students of language need to be aware of the impact of syntax:

1. The syntax of any given language both demonstrates and controls the thought patterns of its users. That is, as the culture grows, its language grows and shapes accordingly. Likewise structural limitations placed on language by accident or design shape and limit the way its users think.[1] This mutually reinforcing phenomenon is of great concern to cultural anthropologists and psychologists, who compare various languages in order to understand the way thought patterns develop.

2. Imperfections—both in the way a language is constructed syntactically and in the form it may take in a given utterance—may produce ambiguity.

Ambiguity. Although one speaks loosely of ambiguous situations and contexts, we shall regard ambiguity as a property of language. More specifically, ambiguity is the capacity of a given piece of language to mean more than one thing. Do not confuse this capacity with the ability to be unclear. This we call "vagueness."[2] Thus, "I feel blah!" is vague: The word "blah" has a great range and variety of interpretations. "The tape recorder with the foot pedal which I bought yesterday" is ambiguous. I may have bought the complete set yesterday or I may have purchased the tape recorder earlier and the foot pedal

[1] See George Orwell, **1984** (New York: Harcourt, Brace and Co., 1949).
[2] Max Black, **Critical Thinking: An Introduction to Logic and Scientific Method** (New York: Prentice-Hall, Inc., 1946), pp. 168–169.

attachment yesterday. Thus the distinguishing factor of ambiguity is that the meanings are **clear**—only the **choice** is in question.

Examples of syntactical ambiguity are common and mostly they cause no trouble. The "Lady from Pasadena" story is by now legendary. Her original ad went something like this: "For sale: grand piano by retired Pasadena schoolteacher with solid oak legs." If you have filled out a job application form recently you may have paused over an instruction which said: "Please check your sex." And if you are old enough to remember the days when the purple people eater roamed the land, you may recall wondering whether you were to fear some kind of purple monster who ate people or an equally improbable eater of purple people.

Such examples have for centuries been a source of dubious hilarity; and one wonders if their study is worth the bother. But other syntactically ambiguous assertions are more difficult to detect and more serious in consequence. When I say, "It is unwise for a speaker to ask his audience for overt action in the middle of a speech," what is it that is not supposed to happen in the middle of the speech: the overt action or the request for overt action? And when a press release states: "Yesterday allied forces firing from five miles offshore for the first time damaged communist shore batteries," what was it that happened for the first time: the firing from five miles offshore or the damaging of shore batteries? Attorneys are quick to affirm that syntactical ambiguity can make a monumental difference when a claim is being settled or a will brought to probate.

You may have noticed that the above examples—with one exception —illustrate ambiguity caused by **syntactical** factors. But by our definition of "ambiguity," syntax is only one cause of ambiguous assertions. Much commoner is the ambiguity which springs from a single word. When I say "My dog has a tremendous appetite and he is very fond of children," my assertion is clearly ambiguous. Equally clearly, syntax has nothing to do with the ambiguity. The word "fond" is the culprit. The same situation occurs when someone says, "She acted funny" and we wonder "funny—ha-ha" or "funny—strange"? This brings us to the huge question of how words mean—our real meat for this chapter.

Semantic meaning

We have already seen how words must go together in certain ways in order to make sense. The next step would seem to be a close look at words themselves—how many kinds there are and how they mean. But you may remember from the introduction how, out of all the words we produce and consume, only a handful seem to be tied directly to the world we are talking about. We also noted that it frequently took a large and strange assortment of words bundled together to name a single feature in the outside world. These phenomena would seem to provide two good reasons for us to swear off words entirely and devote our attention to word bundles; that is, to collections of words which name the things we want to talk about, and to other collections which we use to talk about them. But lest some of us be still addicted to the single word, there is a third and compelling reason why word-by-word study will not do. In order to fully understand this third problem we must list the kinds of words in the English language as given to us by traditional grammar:

Noun	Adjective
Pronoun	Preposition
Verb	Conjunction
Adverb	Interjection

These are the categories, we are sometimes told, into which all words fall. And by so classifying words we can tell how each functions. But even traditional grammarians are fully cognizant that what a word looks like is no necessary indication of how it is going to perform. "Swimming" looks like a verb but when we say "swimming is fun," "swimming" plays the part of a noun. Such deviations from the norm are handled under "exceptions to the general rule." In this case "swimming" is usually called a "gerund." When other parts of speech get into contexts which cause them to behave oddly, other exceptions are formulated.

But you and I are studying the way language relates to the world. And even the complete description of traditional grammar will not help us in some cases. Take the word "neighbor." Clearly a noun, this word seems to place its object in the same group with cats, republicans, and the like. But we can easily go out into the world and distinguish cats from non-cats and—with a little more careful study—Republicans from non-Republicans. When we try to distinguish neighbor from non-neighbor, what are we to look for? A little thought shows us that a man cannot be a neighbor by himself, but only in relation to somebody else. Thus the word "neighbor," though noun in form, functions in a relative way and should probably be rendered "neighbor of." This distinction may seem obvious or petty; but it becomes crucial later on when we analyze such statements as "every American should have the right to choose his own neighbor."

What we have said in effect is that, as it was with paragraphs and sentences, so it is with individual words: The form is no guarantee of the function. And before we get involved in the modest task of trying to classify everything in the world one might want to talk about, we must introduce a new notion.

The designator concept

We noted earlier that "the tall man standing on the patio with a brief-case in his hand" refers to only one individual—though it took thirteen words to fix upon him. Later when we know him better we may call him "Sam." He is still the same man, but his thirteen-word name has been reduced to one. If we are going to make any sense out of all of this we must take our attention away from the parts of speech in that thirteen-word phrase and concentrate on what it means. And since words will, in every instance of naming or describing, go together in different packages, we need a name for such packages regardless of their context. We choose the name "designator," by which we mean any word or group of words which in a given context names or describes.

The idea of predication. Before stopping to quarrel with the ad-mittedly loose way we have defined "designator" we should draw back and look once again at the way we use language to talk about the world. If we return to our friend with the briefcase who is waiting pa-tiently on the patio, we note that the original thirteen-word phrase made no claim; it merely fixed upon an individual. If we rephrase the formulation as follows: "The tall man with the briefcase **is** standing on the patio," we have now indicated the object of our discourse with six words and have used the remaining words to say something about him. Note the subtle introduction of the word "is" here. "Is" is used in many ways; here it functions as what we call a **"predicator"**—that is, it helps the last part of the formulation to make claim about the in-dividual named in the first part. In English "is" is not always needed to predicate. We can as easily say "John runs" as "John is running." In fact, "is" never predicates by itself (except in rare instances to claim existences, as in "God is"). Normally it takes "is," plus some other words to predicate (make claims). The kinds of words used for predication will be studied closely in just a moment. First, we must look at the kinds of language needed to **indicate** the thing about which we wish to talk.

Indicators

Individual designators. The people, things, and events in the world we call "individuals." The designators we use to refer to them are called "individual designators." If all the people, things, and events in the world had names, and if we all knew all the names, life would be a good deal simpler. As it is, most of the people, some of the things, and a few of the events in the world have names; but even these names are known to only a fraction of those who want to talk about them. The tall man standing on my patio surely has a name. But I don't know what it is so I designate him as merely "the tall man with the briefcase."

Notice the difference between these two indicating processes. "Ralph Waldo Emerson," "The White House," "July 4, 1776" name respectively a person, a thing, and an event. The names are relatively well known in the English-speaking community. If I wish to refer to any of these individuals I need only to utter the appropriate name. "The man with the briefcase," "the third tree from the left in the garden," "the sinking of the Titanic" indicate the same kinds of individuals; but in this case no names are handy, and we must do the best we can in putting language together to refer our listener or reader to the desired piece of the world. Such word collections are often called "descriptive phrases," identifiable not by the number or kinds of words they contain, but by the fact that they combine to indicate—to focus attention upon—that which we would discuss.

The descriptive phrase is a strange mechanism of language and merits a closer scrutiny than we have given it. When I say "the present President of the United States," almost any speaker of English knows whom I mean. But what happens when I say "The present King of Mexico?" To whom does this bit of language refer? Each of the individual words in this descriptive phrase is a common one; and the meaning of each is well understood. Any reasonably literate speaker of English knows what "present" and "king" and "Mexico" refer to. Each of these words can make sense when alone. But somehow when we put the three together they combine to indicate something we can **con**ceive but cannot **per**ceive—it simply isn't there. When language combines to indicate something which we are sure we would recognize but which we are equally sure doesn't exist in this world, we call such language a **partial designator.** The phenomenon of partial designation will be treated in greater detail after we've had a look at designators of classes.

Class designators. Probably the most misunderstood language we encounter is the designator of a class (a group of individuals displaying a common characteristic). Such names as "bird" and "tree" indeed seem simple enough. All we have to do is agree as to what they mean or, if in doubt, look them up in a dictionary. The first shock occurs when we try to link these common bits of language—usually nouns or noun phrases—to the bits of the world they designate, and find nothing there! For though there are plenty of trees and birds around, we can nowhere find bird or tree. These exist only in our minds. Somewhere along the way we noted similar features in individual birds and coined the word "bird" to cover all such creatures—even those which have not yet come into the world.

Thus are classes indestructible. We could kill all the birds in the world, or burn up all the trees; but in the process we would do no damage to the classes themselves. These would go right on as long as there were people to think of them.

How are classes indicated? We already noted the common noun which names so many of the classes in our everyday experiences. But are we to invent a new name every time we conceive a new class?

Earlier we mentioned "the President of the United States" as indicating an individual. But what about this sentence: "The President of the United States is Commander-in-Chief of the Armed Forces"? Here we mean not just the present President but anyone who occupies this office—conceivably an infinite class. So apparently the descriptive phrases which we identified earlier as individual indicators may indicate classes as well. You may remember from the "Get Tough" passage in Chapter One that lengthy descriptive phrase, "those who are bent on destroying our country by senseless rioting." This is a class designator; that is, when and if we learn what the author means by it we shall have established the limits of a definite class: To be a member one must be bent on destroying our country by senseless rioting—whatever that is. (When we come to examine this class for members we may be in for a second shock.) First we must distinguish two kinds of meaning for class designators: **denotative** versus **connotative** meaning. But be warned; semanticists have found it necessary to deviate from the traditional "denotation" and "connotation." If you have been accustomed to using these words in a special way you will want to make careful note of the definitions given below.

A. **Denotation.** The denotation of a designator,[3] sometimes called "referent" or "designation," is the external entity to which the designator refers. From this it follows that we cannot speak or write the denotation of a designator; we can only point to it or depict it or refer to it. If one asks, "What is the denotation of 'pig'?" no reply can **be** the denotation itself. The denotation of "pig" is a class of animals, and cannot be uttered or written.

B. **Connotation.** The connotation of a designator is the sum total of properties implied in its meaning and in its understanding by a consumer. Immediately a distinction is necessary:

1. **Objective (informative) connotation.** The objective connotation of a designator is that portion of its meaning which is normally found in its dictionary definition. Thus the informative connotation of "snipe" is: "a shot from a hidden position" **(American College Dictionary, 1951, p. 1143).** The fact that the word "snipe" may have several distinct meanings does not affect the concept of objective connotation. "Snipe" meaning a shot from a hidden place and "snipe" meaning a kind of bird may be the same word **but it is not the same designator!** There are as many designators as there are things referred to; thus a word may have many informative connotations, but a designator has only one.

2. **Subjective (affective) connotation.** In addition to the objective connotation which every designator can be expected to have for all who use it, there will inevitably attach to any designator additional meanings (called collectively "subjective connotation") which obviously will vary from one consumer to another. "Pig" to a farmer may connote "bacon, market, so much per pound," while to a city dweller it may suggest "ugh! dirty, sleeps in mud, fat and sloppy." Few words are used repeatedly in a language without developing some degree of subjective connotation.

Having noted how class designators have at least two kinds of meaning (denotative and connotative) we are now better situated to deal with a word like "unicorn." Clearly this word indicates a class—horses

---

[3] Note that denotation and objective connotation are properties of designators, not (necessarily) of individual words.

with horns—and equally clearly there are none! A close look at the language reveals a surprising number of words and groups of words designating things one doesn't seem to find in the world. You may have noticed a similarity between such class indicators and the individual "present King of Mexico," discussed earlier. These are instances of **partial designation,** a phenomenon so deceptive and so far-reaching in its consequences that a second look is in order.

Partial designators.   The word "cat" has meaning for us as a class of physical entities (its denotation) and also in terms of the properties it suggests (its connotation). The word "unicorn" however, can only connote, it denotes nothing. We know what a unicorn would be if there were one, but there aren't any. Thus "unicorn" is a partial designator; it has connotation but no denotation.

Here one must distinguish between the partial and the vague. It is tempting to say "love" is a partial designator because nobody knows exactly what it means. But this is precisely what a partial designator is not. To be partial a designator must connote clearly to us. Only then can we say it has no denotation. But what if we are not sure, as with "flying saucer"? Once we get this designator shaken down so that its connotation is precise we are still in doubt as to the denotation. And to return to that long, cumbersome class indicator from the "Get Tough" passage, "those who are bent on destroying our country with senseless rioting," we may even here be wise to question the existence of denotative meaning. There no doubt are people who are bent on destroying our country, and some of them surely are willing to do it by rioting if that seems the best way. But the word "senseless" may mean "purposeless" and this seems to contradict the metaphor "bent" in the earlier part of the designator. In short by the time we get this monstrous class indicator unscrambled and find out in whose view the rioting must be senseless, we may find the club so exclusive that nobody belongs! In this case we would say that the designator is **partial,** having connotation but no denotation.

So far we have looked mainly at class indicators as examples of partial designation. Let's not forget the "present King of Mexico." Partial designators are in fact of two types: (1) indicators of classes without members and (2) indicators of individuals that don't exist. It should further be noted that for both the class and individual, partial designation is usually accomplished through the descriptive phrase rather than the individual designator. Words such as "unicorn" are not nearly so prevalent as phrases like "that scandal in Washington" or "the predisposition of Republicans to ignore the common man" or "the collapse of the Vietnamese army." For it is no trick to put language together so that it means things that aren't out there. And with the current knowledge explosion many of today's designators may connotate what tomorrow will be seen not to be. "The edge of the world" was a perfectly good designator a few centuries back.

What are we to do with partial designators? Surely we cannot leave them as they are, knowing (or suspecting) that what they name isn't there. Perhaps the answer lies in the closeness of the meaning problem to the questions of truth, something beyond our purview. If I say, "The man standing in the hall is my brother," and there is in fact no man standing in the hall I have plainly uttered a partial designator. Had I said, "There is a man standing in the hall and he is my brother," I should have uttered not a partial designator but a lie—deliberate or inadvertent. So apparently the best way to handle a partial designator is to **rewrite it in the form which reveals the hidden assertion**—that is, in statement form. Thus, "The present scandal in Washington is causing concern among key legislators" becomes "There is a scandal in Washington" and "This scandal is causing concern among key legislators." Thus the claim of scandal, hidden in the original partial designator, is laid bare for all to see. This procedure also takes care of cases where we're not sure whether a given designator has denotation. When in doubt we merely restate the designation in statement form, leaving room for further investigation to reveal the truth or falsity of the claim.

So far we have talked about class designators casually as though the things they named were really the things we wanted to talk about. Thus when we use the common noun "cat," unless we say "this cat" or "the cat in the corner" we are presumably talking about the class of cats. But if you read carefully the definition of "class" given earlier, you were probably troubled by the fact that a class is an abstract entity and the things we say about it usually apply, not to this abstraction, but to the individual members of the class. When one says "cars are expensive" one clearly refers not to the class of the cars (which cannot be bought or sold) but rather to each specific member of that class, or perhaps to the typical member.[4] Almost always when

---

[4] "For any x, if x is a car, x is expensive," from Alfred North Whitehead and Bertrand Russell, **Principia Mathematica,** 2nd ed. (Cambridge: At the University Press, 1925).

we seem to be talking about a class we are actually talking about its members. This confusion is caused by a structural defect in English and often leads to problems such as the following:

I am looking for a girl with blonde hair and blue eyes.

Who (or what) am I looking for? Perhaps I am missing a little sister and wish to identify her to someone who may have seen her passing by. Or maybe I want to get married and will settle for any (or almost any) blue-eyed blonde. There is no way to tell which meaning is intended when one consumes the sentence in isolation. Of course the complete context would undoubtedly reveal the intended meanings. As indicated, this phenomenon is due to a defect in the English language, where one syntactical form must do the job for two separate and distinct meanings. Such ambiguity could never occur in Spanish.[5]

A second and more threatening consequence of this linguistic defect is often loosely called **generalizing.** In this verbal orgy one proceeds lightly from "cars are expensive" to "Jews are stingy" and "Negroes are lazy" and "Birchers are sick." Such assertions give us the comfort of logs on the fire; and obviate any further thinking on the matter. When challenged on the meaning or validity of such an assertion its producer usually replies, "Well, maybe not always, but as a general rule."

Strangely, a widening recognition of this linguistic fallacy has resulted in a pendular swing to an opposite and equally dangerous position in which the semantically astute admonish "you can't generalize." But generalize is what most of us do much of the time; and generalize we must if we are to survive! When I say "iron expands when heated" I am generalizing—and the resulting generalization is a useful piece of knowledge with probability approaching one hundred percent. Thus the problem would **seem** to be one of truth or validity rather than meaning, and thus totally out of place in the study of semantics.

The roots of this problem, however, are imbedded more in semantics than in logic. For the original error occurred when we thought we could say things like "expensive" and "lazy" about classes at all. Once we get it clear in our heads that it is not the classes we are talking

---

[5] Compare: "Busco un hombre que hable Espanol."
　　　　　"Busco **a** un hombre que habla Espanol."
Both are translated: "I am looking for a man who speaks Spanish," but the first refers to any man, the second to a specific individual.

about but rather its individual members—people and things—then the problem disappears. As footnoted earlier, the "for any x" formulation forces thought away from the class and onto its members. But few of us can be persuaded to inject x's and y's into our everyday discourse. Probably the only answer is for us to go on making such general statements (most of us will anyway) but, through understanding the basic difference between a class and its members, to be fully aware of what we are doing. And in consuming such generalized discourse there can be no substitute for the constant, rigorous determination of the precise nature of the claim being made.

Abstraction. Having bundled neatly into classes anything one might wish to talk about, we should not be surprised that a few items have been left out. What, for example, shall we do with "truth" and "beauty"? These are hardly classes with individual members. And yet we often have occasion to talk about them. Our answer lies in the fact that we do not find truth and beauty alone in the world around us. Short of metaphysics, we find truth attached to statements of ideas and beauty to things and concepts. When we speak of truth and beauty separate from that which is true and beautiful, we are abstracting. That is, we are pulling out an aspect of something—or of many things —and shining a spotlight on it.[6] Abstractions such as "truth," "beauty," "loneliness" are an important part of our language and are usually regarded as a special kind of class.

Our discussion of indicators (individual and class designators) has led us into some rather intricate detail; but the undertaking was scarcely a modest one. One could hardly hope to categorize everything worth talking about with names for each, without running into some snags. It is now our lot to examine the language used to predicate about the world we have indicated. In other words, having blandly uncovered the machinery for naming everything in sight or mind, we now look at language used to make claims, to say—to assert.

Predicators

Property designators. When we first talked about classes we said they were composed of individuals exhibiting a common characteristic. You may have noticed that the word "characteristic" was left conveniently

[6] Hubert G. Alexander, **Language and Thinking: A Philosophical Introduction** (Princeton, N. J.: D. Van Nostrand Company, Inc., 1967), chap. 5.

undefined. We are now ready to formalize that notion with the word "property." Properties are found attached to other things, usually to individuals—they are never found by themselves. When a single word designates a property it is usually an adjective or an intransitive verb (for example: "green," "running"). Often, however, as with the descriptive phrases which name individuals and classes, we find properties designated by groups of words (examples: "is running swiftly," "is capable of being verified"). In the statement, "This sentence is capable of being verified," "this sentence" indicates the individual we are talking about and "capable of being verified" designates the property. Note the function of "is" in linking the indicator to its predicator.

What about adverbs? Do they predicate properties? When we say "John is running swiftly," is "swiftly" a property? If so, a property of what? Language analysts vary in their approach to this problem; but for our purposes it will be best to regard the entire phrase "is running swiftly" as a property predicated of John. It may be objected that, if John is actually running slowly, then the entire property predicator "is running swiftly" is both true and false at the same time. This should cause little difficulty, however. As soon as it is determined what "swiftly" means in this context (that is, how fast one must run in order to be running swiftly) the entire predicated property will be understood and may be adjudged true or false. If you have been brought up on traditional grammar you may find this way of thinking awkward. But bear with it—it will pay big dividends later!

The next question is: What kind of things do we find properties attached to? We said casually "usually individuals." But what about classes? Are there properties of classes? This question revives the problem which troubled us a while back. In predicating the property of expensiveness to the class of cars we found it wasn't the class at all that was expensive but rather its members. And while it is common and permissible to say "cars are expensive," predicating a property of the class of cars, we must keep ever in mind that it is not the abstract class itself we are talking about.

Classes do, however, have certain properties—not expensiveness or greenness, but rather size, inclusiveness, and the like. The same is true of properties and relations. We sometimes predicate properties of them; but such properties are normally of interest only to logicians and semanticists. The rule of thumb that properties are predicated of individuals is a good one to follow.

Did you pause over "John is running" as an example of property predication? Perhaps you felt that "John is red-headed" (or, more precisely, red-haired) exemplified a more permanent property. The attempt to separate permanent from temporary properties, however, breaks down in practice. In this material world nothing is permanent; and the fact that John's red hair will last longer than his running is irrelevant in language study. It is better, then, to treat all properties—the relatively permanent and the relatively temporary—in the same way.

Finally, if properties are the deciding elements by which individuals are bundled into classes, aren't classes and properties really the same thing? That is, when I say "John is a Republican," am I predicating a property or class membership? The difference is technical and not very important to us at the moment. Arbitrarily we say that we are predicating properties in all cases. (It would be awkward to say "John is a member of the class of all beings which are running at the moment.") And if under this definition you are tempted to conclude that predicating properties is just about all we do all day long, you are urged to defer final judgment until you have studied relations.

Relation designators. Like properties, relations attach themselves to things. The difference is: Relations tie together two or more of these things. A relation is meaningless without the two (or more) items it relates, yet, it is a property of neither. Relations are normally designated by prepositions, transitive verbs, and by special symbols not included in the parts-of-speech system. For example:

under   is taller than   likes   ÷ (divided by)

The first thing one notices about relation designators is that there are not enough of them. Adjectives and intransitive verbs pretending to designate properties have stolen the show. Consider for example the word "moves" and some of its related verbiage ("stands still," "stationary," "motion"). This varied collection, of intransitive verb, adverb, adjective, and noun, surely suggests a property—that is, motion would seem to be at a given moment a property of some objects and not of others. But a careful glance at the world around us reveals what is common knowledge to any physicist: No object can be examined for its motion or lack of it except in comparison with some other object taken as stationary. Centuries of using the earth's surface (or something attached to it) as the basis for measuring motion or stillness has built a vocabulary of property designators to refer to what is actually a relation. Scientists and technicians have invented special symbols to overcome this linguistic aberration. But the rest of us are stuck. If we want to be precise we must remember to say "X moves (or is still) **with respect to Y.**" This way we reveal what an intransitive verb has tried to hide—that motion is relative.

A similar case in point is our old friend "neighbor." A noun by any standard, "neighbor" seems to indicate a class. But as we noted earlier, you can look at a man in isolation and see that he is redheaded, bespectacled, etc., but where do you find his neighbor-ness? Clearly a man is a neighbor only in relation to someone or something outside himself; and the accurate formulation should be X **neighbor of** Y. The enormous significance of this noun-which-hides-a-relation will be seen in just a moment.

Next to note about relations is that many of them carry unexpected consequences. Cohen and Nagel[7] cite these consequences in the form of properties of relations essentially as follows:

Reflexivity.   A relation is reflexive when an object bears the relation not to some other object but to itself. The identity relation is the typical example: A thing is identical with itself; X is identical with X.

Transitivity.   A relation is transitive if, when an object bears it to a second object which in turn bears it to a third, then the first object must bear this relation to the third. Example: "Taller than." (If John is taller than Jim and Jim is taller than Bob, then John must be taller than Bob.)

Reciprocity.   A relation is reciprocal if, when an object bears it to another object, the second must bear the same relation to the first. Example: "married to." (If John is married to Mary, then Mary must be married to John.)

Note that the relation "brother of" is transitive but not reciprocal. That is, if X is brother of Y and Y is brother of Z, X must be brother of Z (transitivity); but if X is the brother of Y, Y need not be the brother of X (reciprocity). Note also that the relation "neighbor of," cited earlier as an example of a common noun concealing a relation, turns out on examination to be reciprocal. That is, assuming some kind of spatial or residential meaning for "neighbor," X cannot be neighbor of Y without Y being neighbor of X as well. It seems the simple common noun "neighbor" hides more complexities than one might imagine.

[7] Cohen, Morris, and Ernest Nagel, **Introduction to Logic and Scientific Method** (New York: Harcourt, Brace & World, 1934).

What about such designators as "and," "or," and "implies"? Do these not designate relations? Logicians sometimes refer to these as "logical connectors" serving usually to relate not things but sentences. While it is true that in "John and Mary are singing a duet," "and" links John and Mary in an activity which neither is performing by himself, this function of "and" is the exception rather than the rule. Usually when the conjunction relates two classes or individuals it is actually functioning as a shorthand way of writing two sentences. Thus "John and Tom are Democrats" might more precisely be written "John is a Democrat and Tom is a Democrat." Likewise, "He will come today or tomorrow" means "He will come today or he will come tomorrow." The function of a conjunctive relation designator as a connector between sentences is of special interest to the semanticist, as will be indicated when we discuss evaluative conjunctions.

Expressors

With the world as complicated as it is, we have done well to keep the categories of language used to describe it down to manageable size. If we were to open the door to all language not used for descriptive purposes, many more notions would have to be introduced. What would we do, for example, with such language as "hurray" and "ouch"? We already know how to translate such fragments when, despite their exclamatory form, they are obviously cognitive in function[8] (for example: "Ouch!" meaning, "You are standing on my foot."). But when such language is used exclusively for expressive purposes it is called "expressive language" or "expressors." Such words as "hurray" do not designate at all but rather express. That is, the word "approval" **designates** approval; "hurray" **expresses** approval. When such expressors appear in language with cognitive intent they are eliminated in translation.

If you find yourself bewildered with the linguistic intricacies of this chapter, draw back for a moment and remember what we set out to do in the first place. The whole of descriptive language, we said, was one set of words clustering in groups to name things and another set of words saying something about these things. The fact that individual words function differently almost every time they are used should

---

[8] See Chapter Three.

alert us more than ever to the need to study each statement on its own, trying to see how language is used in each case to indicate something and to say something about it.

Applications

For the public speaker. Get a copy of a model speech (perhaps one of your own) and isolate a paragraph of particularly weighty substance. You will probably find that the indicators are long and involved, that the speaker has taken many words to indicate the class or individual he wants to talk about. While this does not necessarily make for bad composition, you will find in most cases that these classes or individuals can be designated by simpler language. If rewriting these indicators in simpler language changes the meaning somewhat, examine the context carefully and see whether the assertion can more safely and accurately be made of the original or of the revised version. For example, try some one word replacements for "Those who are bent on destroying our country by senseless rioting," and note the impact on the overall meaning.

Next turn your attention to those places in the speech (if any) where properties seem to be predicated of classes. (Example: "Russians are inclined to be disinterested in politics.") Note the difference in impact when one thinks of the property as predicated of each individual member of the class. Where appropriate, try to assign a percentage or probability on the basis of which you think the author would be justified in generalizing for the entire class. (How many Russians must be disinterested in politics for the above-quoted sentence to be true?)

For the debater. In this chapter we saw how "neighbor," though a common noun, actually predicates a relation ("neighbor of")—and a reciprocal relation at that. Assume that you are debating the proposition: "Resolved: that everyone should have the right to choose his own neighbor." Regardless of which side you find yourself on, consider the impact of the following analysis on the course of the argument:

Analysis:
I don't know exactly what it is to choose one's own neighbor. (The **meaning** of the proposition is in doubt.)
Observation:
A neighbor is not a thing at all but rather a relationship between two people or families—in this case, a residential relationship. The

exact distance between residences isn't important—we can settle that later.

Analysis:

"Neighbor of" predicates a reciprocal relationship. That is, X neighbor of Y must imply Y neighbor of X.

Observation:

Then it's impossible for everyone to have the right to choose his own neighbor; for due to the reciprocity of "neighbor of," each choice must be mutual by the chooser and the chosen. In fact, one rarely chooses one's residential neighbor. I don't think we are talking about choosing at all, but rather about **excluding** as neighbor certain persons or members of certain groups.

Analysis:

The relation designated by "excludes as neighbor" is also reciprocal, that is, if X excludes Y as neighbor Y must (deliberately or perforce) exclude X.

Observation:

For everyone to have the right to exclude anyone else as neighbor, two persons or families will be neighbors only by mutual consent. Maybe if we start here the argument will get somewhere.

Summary

Syntactical meaning results from the way words go together in a sentence. Ambiguity occurs when two or more clear cut meanings are possible. Semantic meaning occurs when individual words in a given context work together as designators to name and talk about the world. Those designators which perform the naming function are called **"indicators"** (individual and class designators); those which say something about the things indicated are called **"predicators"** (property and relation designators).

Questions and exercises

1. Locate the syntactical ambiguity in each of the following:
   a. A speaker should not ask his audience for overt action in the middle of a speech.
   b. Radicals have worked great mischief; neither the Socialists nor the Democrats can undo the damage they have done.
   c. Without remorse the colored window washer strangled the girl with the rope necklace.

d. I am looking for a girl with blonde hair and blue eyes.

Rewrite each sentence to express unambiguously each possible meaning. How many rewrites are needed for (b) ? for (c) ? What is responsible for the ambiguity in (d) ?

2. Underline the linguistic symbols; then circle the designators; then check (✔) any designator without denotation (partial designator):

     whew!   or   the sixth Tuesday in March
     duck soup   is   under the tree

3. Divide the first sentence of the "Get Tough" passage into designators, labeling each "class," "individual," "property," or "relation." Remember, several words may combine to comprise one designator.

4. In the following excerpt, **circle** any designators which are (or may be) partial.

Los Angeles, February 30:

    In asking State College faculty how soon they could be ready for the coming change to the quarter system, the Chancellor showed an awareness of the faculty's reluctance to make a change. His inquiry as to whether the advantages of the quarter system would justify the red tape involved, merely underline this awareness. Indeed, the original Chancellor's Report of 1944 had predicted this reluctance on the part of the faculty. Thus it is surprising that the Coordinating Council, in its demands for a conversion speed-up, has not demonstrated a comparable awareness.

If you find yourself circling nearly all the indicators, it is because (not knowing the context) you can't know whether most of the items referred to actually exist. And did you remember to circle "February 30"?

FIVE

The language of value

To this point we have considered the various ways in which language may be meaningful, and have studied ways to reduce to referential statements all language which may be cognitive in function. In the previous chapter we looked at the internal components of these referential statements—designators—and at how they could go together to make sense. This would seem to be the end of the matter as far as meaning is concerned. But a moment's reflection shows us that all that **looks** descriptive (referential) may not be so. Remember that elusive tautology from Chapter Two? On the surface it looked like a referential statement. Only when we examined the tautology's function did we discover that it claimed nothing at all about the world. Further examination of presumably referential language reveals that much of it approves or disapproves while pretending to describe. So prevalent and intriguing is this feature of our language that we must devote an entire chapter to careful study of the evaluative assertion.

The nature of evaluation

Let us for the moment define "evaluative" as "expressive of approval or disapproval." Thus an evaluative assertion is one in which the formulator approves or disapproves of something (or, in rare cases, places that something on the neutral mark of his approval-disapproval continuum). Examples:

John is good.
This is a good book.

With these formulations looking so much like descriptions, how are we to know when the language producer is evaluating? What are the key marks of evaluation? The best answer—and admittedly it doesn't help us much—is given by Carl Wellman:

> Every evaluative sentence is for or against its object in a way that descriptive sentences never are. To evaluate is not to classify an object but to favor or disfavor it. . . . It is this positive or negative feature of partiality which sets evaluative sentences apart from descriptive ones.[1]

This assertion makes a distinction (between descriptive and evaluative language) which is adequate for the purpose of this chapter. But the distinction is purely in terms of **intent** and **effect.** It tells us nothing about the language in which evaluations may be couched. A thorough study of this latter factor is clearly in order.

First we must be aware that, in this age of science and pseudo-science, to be objective and impartially descriptive is thought a fine thing. To allow one's emotions and feelings to intrude into otherwise descriptive discourse is generally regarded with suspicion. Thus it is not surprising that modern vocabulary has built up a rather impressive array of apparently descriptive language. Journalists, whose job it is to report the world to us, are told to be objective—to tell who, what, when, and where, but not to speculate over why, lest their own feelings or emotions intrude on their bland impartiality. Indeed, so widespread is the cult of linguistic objectivity that many of us have to pay huge sums to psychiatrists to drag out of us how we really feel about the world. But our attitudes of approval or disapproval of the things we care about and talk about are ever with us; and much of this approval or disapproval can be identified in the language we use.

This chapter will deal with the many linguistic forms in which our evaluations manage to hide themselves, and with how to restate (for better understanding) in pure form, with the descriptions and evaluations separate and distinct. But before we attempt this, a word of warn-

[1] Carl Wellman, **The Language of Ethics** (Cambridge, Mass.: Harvard University Press, 1961), p. 220.

ing is in order. It will be easier to sense a hidden evaluation than it will be to isolate the precise bit of language which is responsible. And you will find this detective job most difficult when you turn the searchlight on your own discourse, which you may have felt was the epitome of pure objective description.

The good, the bad, and the neutral

> That gun you sold me is no good.
> That was a good shot.
> Too bad about Uncle Jim.
> Good night.
> Good night!

These five examples contain widely diverse uses of "good" or "bad". Their very diversity leads us to wonder what it is we are saying when we say "X is good." Indeed, ethical and aesthetic philosophers have for centuries puzzled over the nature of the good and the beautiful. Fortunately, a thorough investigation of this topic is not required for our purposes. But we do need a quick look at pure evaluation so that we can see what happens when (as they usually do) descriptive and evaluative efforts get all mixed up.

One meaning of "good" is pure preference. When you say "Ice cream is good," you hardly expect an argument. In fact, so widely disparate is human taste, and so acceptable is it to differ from one's neighbor, that instead of "ice cream is good," we are much more likely to say, "I like ice cream." Nobody will shoot you for what you like or dislike. Substitute "spinach" for "ice cream" and you will not be surprised to hear someone answer, "Do you? I hate it!" Even this verbal exchange produces a surprising pleasure. We almost revel in the fact that for once we can take an opposite position from somebody without something being wrong with one of us.

The key to the ice cream and spinach situation is that, within certain cultural limits, we don't **expect** uniformity. Thus no "because" is required. This is why the word "good" doesn't fit very well in this context. But when you say, "That was a good book," the question, "What was good about it?" seems more in order. If the questioner is persistent with his "Why?" he may run you out of becauses to the point where, in exasperation, you reply, "Well, I liked it, that's all!" And suddenly you find you are talking not about the book but about yourself. This is the key break between description and pure evaluation.

Pure value assertions. When we pick pure examples, the distinction seems quite manageable:

A. John is red-headed.   (Descriptive)
B. John is good.   (Evaluative)

It doesn't seem important for the moment whether the formulator arrived at his evaluation through cognition or emotion or both: The fact is that in B he has asserted his evaluation in pure form. The form is called "pure" because it contains no element of description; it voices none of the descriptive predications—if indeed there were any—on which the evaluation may have been based,[2] and the distinction between it and the description above it seems clear-cut. The one gives a partial description of an object; the other expresses some sort of approval of the object. That John is red-headed can be verified by direct examination of the object (John) without recourse to any outside factors. **But no examination of John can reveal his goodness;** it exists somehow **between** his character (the sum of his words, deeds, and predictable behavior) and the approval of the evaluator.

Luckily for us the pure terms "good" and "bad" aren't used much nowadays to evaluate. One is much more likely to use them in one of the innocuous ways illustrated previously. "This gun is no good" is surely based on the way we expect guns to behave. A faulty trigger or peep-sight has probably prompted the disparaging comment, with no attempt being made to judge the ultimate goodness or badness of guns. And since the expected requirements for gun performance have been fairly well fixed in our culture, the statement, "That gun is no good," is ultimately not evaluative at all but descriptive, since the gun may be measured against universal standards. But even though this universal good is a far cry from the approval-disapproval concept we started with, it is still standard practice to refer to statements like "This gun is no good" as evaluative rather than descriptive.

The absolute versus the relative. On occasion one may hear two

---

[2] Note that this "pure" classification does not require that the assertion have no descriptive **function,** merely that there be no description perceivable in the assertion itself. "John brushes his teeth regularly" (descriptive) may be among the thoughts of the speaker who says, "John is good"; but no description is present in the evaluation itself.

persons, both of whom have read a given book, argue (?) over its merits. One must in this case distinguish contentions concerning the wisdom or validity of certain standards for books (a value-matter) from contentions purporting to measure the book against these standards (a fact-matter). But this argument cannot long survive without "good" and "bad" becoming "better than" or "worse than." For by most evaluative standards no book is completely good or bad. So we must recognize within pure value assertion a distinction between **absolute**— the kind we've talked about so far—and **relative.**

Relative value assertions.

> Brand X is better than brand Y.
> I like strawberry better than vanilla.
> It is better to be safe than sorry.
> Hate is inferior to love.
> Better Red than dead.

Note that these assertions, though they compare one item with another, do not describe either. Note also that the relations "better than" and "worse than" often blur in everyday syntax to "better" and "worse," seeming to predicate properties: "I feel better," "Brand 'X' tastes better," "The weather is worse." (Participants in group discussion should be alert to keep the unexpressed term in mind—" . . . better than what?"—even though demagogues and professional salesmen may strive to keep it hidden.) But regardless of this persistent syntactical slip, relative value assertions are easily identified when they occur in pure form (unmixed with description).

Remarkably, these pure evaluations—whether relative or absolute —cause us little trouble. We may not know precisely what the producer means by his evaluation. But at least we know that he is evaluating. It is right there in plain sight; the words "good" and "bad" (and their equivalents or near-equivalents) always tip us off. But you were warned near the beginning of this chapter that the average speaker and writer of English likes to mix description and evaluation in one innocent-looking assertion. When this happens a host of new problems arise.

Mixed evaluations

When an assertion describes and approves (or disapproves) in the same breath we call it a "mixed evaluation." By this we mean that its producer is telling us something (making a claim) about a portion of the world and at the same time—sometimes obviously, sometimes subtly—praising or deriding what he has described. So skilled have we become in burying our evaluations in the respectable objectivity of descriptive discourse, we often find it next to impossible to ferret out exactly where the evaluation has taken place—especially when it is our own discourse and evaluation. But it is altogether crucial that we learn to do this. For if descriptive discourse is to be of any value, someone must ultimately verify it. And since we do not yet know how to verify evaluations (indeed, their very nature may preclude verification) we must learn to separate the ingredients of the mixed evaluations.

Evaluation by subjective connotation. You will remember from Chapter Four a discussion of connotation as a property of class designators. While we are not in a position to argue the extension of connotation to other kinds of designators, it seems obvious that **subjective connotation**—that which varies from one person to another—may attach itself to any kind of language. Indeed it is nearly impossible for any normal user of a language to avoid developing feeling about a designator he uses regularly. Not all of this subjective connotation expresses approval or disapproval. But where it does we say the designator is "slanted." And it is important that we identify such slanted language and—for the moment at least—separate it from any description it may be attached to. For example:

Jew	Stubborn
Nigger	Fussy
Wop	Crackpot
Scab	
Fuzz	

An obvious question: How do we know when a given word or group of words is slanted? Who decides? Maybe "Jew" is completely neutral to me, even though it isn't to someone else. The honest answer is: We have to guess. We can run a test[3] for any given word, to determine whether a random audience perceives it favorably or unfavorably. But even without a test most of us would be willing to bet on the result with a word such as "nigger." In most cases experience will tell us when a given designator will produce almost universal negative connotation along with its description.

[3] Charles E. Osgood, George J. Suci, and Percy H. Tannenbaum, **The Measurement of Meaning** (Urbana, Ill.: University of Illinois Press, 1957), p. 76.

Noteworthy also is the fact that the words listed in the left hand column above name classes, while those on the right designate properties ("crackpot" may designate either a class or a property). But note that each of these eight words has an **objective** meaning. The trick is to find language which will designate the class or property intended, but which will for a given audience convey little or none of the slant exhibited in the original. Let's look briefly at each of these words.

Linguistic evolution has failed to come up with a neutral equivalent of "Jew." Indeed, we have had so much trouble sorting out the legitimate objective meanings of this indicator (a member of an ethnic group, a cultural group, a religious sect), and keeping these separate from the Mediterranean racial characteristics commonly associated with many Jews, that probably not much thought has been given to a universal neutral substitution. Perhaps the best the language analyst can do with this word is to note carefully the context in which it occurs and to allow for the almost inevitable evaluative connotation.

Until recently "nigger" was the number one word for casting aspersions on the Negro race. "Negro" showed respect and was the proper neutral substitution for "nigger." One of the remarkable linguistic developments of the '60's has been the emergence of the term "black." It seems some of the more thoughtful blacks discovered (or popularized what they had always known) that "Negro," while probably preferable to "nigger," had its own connotation of inferiority and subservience, plus a host of innuendos which most black Americans were fed up with. At this writing "Negro" is acceptable to these blacks only in certain historical contexts. And demeaning connotations long associated with "Negro" by racist Americans (black and white alike) are being counteracted by such phrases as "black is beautiful."

"Wop" is a little-used slur on Italian-Americans, and is easily replaced with the word "Italian." "Scab" refers not to blood clotting on a wound but to a laborer who works for sub-scale wages. The subjective connotation of "scab" must surely be negative; the physical association with the original use of "scab" will see to that. To my knowledge there is no neutral one-word replacement. "Fuzz" as slang for "policeman" was originally a term of contempt. More recently it has been used to include amused tolerance.

The three property predicators in the list exhibit a more transparent mixture. To verbalize the objective portion without the negative connotation one need merely replace "stubborn" with "firm" or "unyielding," "fussy" with "fastidious" or "precise," and "crackpot" with "unorthodox."[4]

Two features of evaluation by subjective connotation should now be apparent. First, it is essentially **environmental** in nature. The designators discussed above acquire whatever evaluative components they possess either from the cultural environment in which they have existed or from the immediate linguistic environment into which they have been thrust. We can, given sufficient skill and vocabulary, replace these mixed value designators with their descriptive equivalents. Whether it takes one word, as with "wop," or several, as with "scab," the result is pure description. Whatever is lost from the original in the replacement process is pure evaluative residue.

A second feature of these evaluators is their **temporal** nature. A word or phrase may become slanted—or unslanted—almost overnight. We saw what happened to "Negro." "Appeasement," as an evaluative variant or "negotiation" in foreign policy, is another example. A time may come when such a procedure as finding out what your neighbor nations want and, consistent with your own genuine needs, giving it to them will no longer call for contempt. At such time "appeasement" will be perceived in this context as a synonym or near-synonym for "negotiation," its negative slanting having been replaced by neutrality or favor. Later we shall study evaluators which (as opposed to the environmental and temporal slanters) have their evaluative component built into their very objective meanings.

A final observation should be made about evaluative subjective connotation and the concept of separation via replacement. You may have enjoyed experimenting with Bertrand Russell's game, and indeed have found surprise and pleasure in your skill, as you merrily substituted "smashed" for "intoxicated," and so on. But the reverse process —finding an exact neutral equivalent for an evaluative designator which may have become an integral part of your vocabulary—is not so easy. Like the innocuous firearm, language is psychologically easier to load than to unload. And finding oneself armed with loaded language, the temptation to open fire is often irresistible.

---

[4] A popular parlor game usually attributed to Bertrand Russell involves conjugating adjectives into three forms, each more progressively negatively oriented. Thus, "firm," "stubborn," and "pigheaded"; "I am precise," "You are fussy," "He is an old woman."

Evaluation by metaphor. You will remember metaphor (Chapter Two) as a special kind of meaning. To take a metaphor literally, we said, would be absurd and unfair to its producer. We then agreed to rewrite metaphors in literal language when we felt the producer intended to make a literal claim. But metaphor may have still another face. On occasion it may cloak its producer's approval or disapproval of the metaphor's object.

A. The President notified the congressional committee that the executive files would no longer be open to committee investigators.	**Description**
B. The President pulled the rug out from under the committee.	**Metaphor** (Mixed evaluative assertion)
A. The new foreign policy precludes the use of nuclear weapons in limited wars.	**Description**
B. The new foreign policy forces the President to fight with one hand tied behind his back.	**Metaphor** (Mixed evaluative assertion)
A. Discontinuation of farm price supports will remove a basic assistance on which the farmer has relied.	**Description**
B. Discontinuation of farm price supports will scuttle the American farmer.	**Metaphor** (Mixed evaluative assertion)

One first notices considerable difference between the "A" and "B" version in each case. Certainly the "B" statements are far from equivalent to the "A"'s. But statements like the "B" examples are common in everyday discourse; and, when asked to clarify, producers usually end up with something like the "A" version. When I asked the producer of the "scuttle the farmer" metaphor what he meant by it he replied, "Just what I said—you would literally scuttle the farmer." The use of the word "literally" suggests that this producer (and probably many others like him) is not even aware that he has made a metaphor, much less that the metaphor is evaluative.

Next one sees that, like connotative evaluation, metaphorical evaluation is essentially environmental. That is, it gets its evaluative loading from the surrounding discourse. One could conceivably speak of scuttling the Mafia or the Viet Cong, in which case "scuttle" would be favorably regarded by most American consumers. And one could surely find a context in which each of these colorful metaphors might be uttered by a producer with no interest in the proceedings. In such a case the environment will have neutralized the metaphor.

How shall we treat these evaluative metaphors? The "A" versions given above have been offered as the descriptive components of the metaphors beneath them. But such components are not always so easy to arrive at; and when verbalized they are usually open to dispute. Nevertheless, we are powerless to make any sense out of "The President pulled the rug out from under the committee" unless we try to extract some kind of literal (descriptive) component. Usually the context will give us enough hint to permit a defensible separation into descriptive and evaluative ingredients. The formulator's approval or disapproval of the described operations comprises the evaluative component.

Now let's reverse the process. Start with the discontinuation of farm price supports, add somebody's disapproval of this action and mix the two into one assertion. The result is a mixed evaluation such as the "scuttle" metaphor above.

Evaluation by hiding the ought. When I first learned arithmetic I was taught never to divide by zero or its equivalent. Such algebraic expressions as "x minus x," I was told, were merely disguised zeros or, in the archaic vocabulary of my teacher, "hiding the ought."

Modern communication has produced another kind of ought-hiding. Indeed the word "ought" (and its near equivalents "should" and "must") form in modern use a strange bridge between the cognitive and directive functions of discourse. And because ought-statements usually provoke a "Why?" producers have devised a remarkable variety of linguistic devices for hiding or implying the ought. Each of these devices appears in an apparently descriptive assertion; but each contains an evaluative component. Let's look at some of the forms in which these mixed evaluations appear.[5]

"-ing." Usually verbs ending in "-ing" appear with helping verbs ("is," "should be," and others) and neutrally predicate properties or relations. You will remember our example, "John is running," in which we said "running" predicated a temporary property of John. But

---

[5] Ought-statements themselves will be considered later.

when the "-ing" verb appears in adjective form—usually before a noun —it may well conceal an evaluation. Consider these examples:

A. ...a receding hairline...
B. ...a disgusting exhibition...

In A, "receding" functions neutrally. Though one may have a strong feeling about the matter, the word "receding" does not reflect it. (What "receding" **does** conceal is a relation: Although "receding" seems to suggest a property of somebody's hairline, one sees that there is no way to examine a hairline for its recedingness without comparing it to the same head a while ago, or with one's expectations regarding hairlines.) But in B, the word "disgusting" is another matter. Here the author is disapproving, often to the virtual exclusion of any description. Disgustingness is plainly no part of the performance; the designator "disgusting" relates the performance to somebody's evaluation of it.

How do we locate the descriptive components of "That was a disgusting exhibition"? If we search the context in which the assertion is uttered we may find such descriptive elements as "the performers moved awkwardly" or "the performers were scantily clad." These are the events which presumably provoked the disgust. The evaluative component may be stated in pure form, such as "the producer of the discourse disapproves." If no descriptive clues are available from the context, one is compelled to guess; and the risk involved in such guessing is obvious. In many cases the producer himself may not know what caused him to be disgusted.

The important point to understand and remember here is the subtle insertion of the producer's values into apparently impartial property predication. Try working into sentences (as adjectives) such verbs as "pleasing" and "disappointing" and you will soon see how easy it is to think of these features as properties of an event rather than what they are: mixtures of what we perceive and how we feel about it.

"-ible" and "-able."   If you are a typically reluctant speller, you probably think of words ending "-ible" or "-able" with pangs of uncertainty. (Is it "defensable" or "defensible"?) You may have wondered why we can't agree to spell them all one way. But the "-ibles" and "-ables" are notable for more than the spelling woes they produce. Consider the following:

malleable	uncomfortable
callable	remarkable
reversible	contemptible
convertible	forcible

The first four seem to cause no trouble. "Malleable" refers to the ability of metals to be pounded into a flat sheet. Certain financial stocks or bonds are said to be callable at a certain time or price. Some jackets are reversible and some cars are convertible. In fact, the "-ible" or "-able" suffix seems to refer to a capacity of some sort, the exact nature of which is indicated by the preceding root.

The word "uncomfortable" should give you a twinge of warning. In the first place, if we follow the suffix rule, "uncomfortable" means "incapable of being comforted." But we know the word normally means something else. And to the extent that comfort is good and discomfort bad, the word "uncomfortable" contains a significant value component.

When we get to "remarkable" the real trouble starts. Again, applying the suffix rule we have "capable of being remarked upon." But anything is **capable** of being remarked upon. When we call something "remarkable" we mean it startled us in some way. This feature of unusualness need not contain a value element (as with "a remarkable change in the weather," where we are completely indifferent to the change, except that it surprised us). But refer to a sprinter's performance as "remarkable" or "remarkable under the circumstances" and you are almost inevitably bestowing praise. "Contemptible" behaves in a similar manner. Anything **may** be held in contempt, but when you refer to something as "contemptible" that means **you** hold it in contempt. And as with "disgusting," you have in one word described whatever it is that aroused your contempt and given your evaluation of it.

"Forcible" presents still another problem. Its meaning is not of course "capable of being forced" but rather "with the use of force." Near the end of the Korean War when United Nations officials objected to "the forcible repatriation of North Korean prisoners," North Korea countered by accusing the U.N. of "forcible screening of prisoners" (asking them whether they wanted to go home). Clearly each side was trying to stigmatize the other as a user of force, with the word "forcible" being applied to any presentation of alternatives.

"-ive." Another suffix which has sneaked into the value ranks is the "-ive" ending. Consider the following:

> expensive
> attractive
> abortive

"Expensive" seems harmless enough. Surely this word hides no approval or disapproval. Though one normally complains with the word, one may brag as well, as with "My wonderful expensive fur coat." But "expensive," like the other words we've studied in this section, seems to predicate a property. And yet when you say "That car is expensive," you are fully aware that no examination of the car can reveal its expensiveness. A car—or any other item—is expensive only in terms of what one expects to pay. And it is surprising how rapidly expectation can shift to desire, and expensiveness be predicated on the basis of outrage, regardless of expectation.

When one attributes attractiveness (to a person, say, or a job offer) one is clearly describing certain features and approving of them. Thus "attractive" fits our notion of mixed description and evaluation. "Abortive"[6] is usually predicated of movements or ideas which died aborning. An abortive revolution is one that never got off the ground. And while one could conceivably speak neutrally or even favorably of an abortive revolution, the negative connotation associated with the word "abortion" is almost inescapable.

"-ed" and "-ate."

> converted
> perverted
> distorted
> degenerate

"Converted" is neutral. A converted building is not **per se** good or bad. But change the "con" to "per" and you have a different story. A person accused of perverted acts is rarely being praised. One who traditionally commits such acts is called a "pervert," and this is surely not good. Noteworthy is the fact that an act is called "perverted" only in terms of what one expects or finds acceptable. "Distorted" is similarly

---

[6] "Aborted" would probably be more accurate syntactically; but "abortive" is the commonly accepted form.

measured against some norm of expectation or acceptability. "Degenerate" suggests a reversal of the natural evolutionary direction. When we call a certain kind of modern dancing "degenerate" we are describing it, perhaps as something apes might do, and disapproving of it at the same time.

It is time to take an overall look at the many forms we've been considering, and to rediscover their common dependence on what somehow ought to be. The things, people, transactions of the world, are called disgusting, remarkable, attractive, perverted, only in terms of what one expects and wants them to be. Take away these cultural norms and the ought-oriented mixed evaluators lose a portion of their meaning—the evaluative portion. Thus the importance of keeping the constant (descriptive) component separate in thought, even while the producer of the designator seeks to keep it welded to his evaluation.

It is astonishing how easy our language makes it for us to transfer our evaluations so that they seem to be a part of what we are evaluating. Indeed, it seems to be common practice to foist our feelings about a thing onto the thing itself. With such a high premium placed on descriptive objectivity nowadays, these evaluative predications may well reflect an understandable reluctance to admit that our views of a thing are not universally held.

Goal-oriented language. Sometimes the concealed ought takes the form of a goal or standard or objective. Because the goal is presupposed and not stated, the assertion takes on the appearance of pure description.

  A. The Negative Income Tax is a progressive step.
  B. The Negative Income Tax costs too much.
  C. The Negative Income Tax is an important proposal.

The presence of "progressive" in Example A should warn that an evaluation is involved. For though progress is change—which can be measured and described—progress must entail a goal or a set of goals by which the change may be evaluated and declared (more or less) progressive. All instances of change, that is, are not progressive —only those leading in directions or exhibiting criteria deemed by the producer to lead in a desirable direction. This mixed evaluation may be separated into components as follows:

The Negative Income Tax will produce x, y, z.   **(Descriptive)**

Continued absence of the Negative Income Tax   **(Descriptive)**
will produce p, q, r.

x, y, z (the combination) **is better than** p, q, r.   **(Evaluative)**

(Note the use of x's and y's when there is no context to tell us what predictions are implied.)

In Example B the culprit is the adverb "too." If I ask how much the Negative Income Tax will cost annually and someone answers "$18 billion," I have a (predicted) description of an aspect of the Tax: its cost. But what can "too much" mean? How do I examine the Negative Income Tax's predicted cost for suspected too-muchness? Again:

The Negative Income Tax will cost $18 billion.   **(Descriptive)**

Not to spend $18 billion for this purpose is **better**   **(Evaluative)**
than to spend it.

The value component in example C is not immediately apparent. Surely to call the Negative Income Tax "important" isn't to approve or disapprove of its passage. But importance is here predicated, not of its passage, but of the proposal itself. And again, we can examine a proposal for its provisions but not for its importance. The latter is a measure of the proposal against other proposals, or of problems it purports to solve against other problems—all ranked along some important—unimportant continuum known to the producer of the discourse. And in this continuum lies the pure value element: Without it, "important" has limited meaning.

Given that "important" evaluates in this context, does it also describe? Or is the predication of importance nothing more than an expression of pure (relative) preference? Reflection shows the latter to be highly improbable: One doesn't rate Negative Income Tax as more important than (say) Civil Rights legislation in the same way that one prefers asparagus to spinach. In everyday argument, importance is usually predicated of questions or problems the answers to which give our side the edge. (Assume I favor Negative Income Tax and Civil Rights legislation. Candidate "X" is for the former but against the latter; candidate "Y" the reverse. If "X" can't change my mind about Civil Rights he seeks my vote anyway, because "what happens to Negative Income Tax is more important than what happens to Civil Rights legislation.") As a frequent participant in formal or informal discussions you are familiar with such phrases as "The point is . . ." or "The question is . . ." or "That's not the point!"—usually serving to direct attention toward one truth and away from another. Such phrases as "important" and "crucial," then, when used as above, must be included as goal-oriented mixed value language.

Even to exemplify the incredible varieties of goal-oriented language would be too much to do here. "Success," "failure," "proper," "appropriate," "degenerate," "distorted," and "lost" (as in a bargaining session) are but a few. Each of these designators loses a large part of its meaning once the goal or norm is removed. As with "progress," evaluators like "distorted," "improved," and "degenerate," bereft of the implied goal, revert to their parent meaning: change. That is, without a goal by which to measure distortion, improvement or degeneration, all that is left (the descriptive portion) is change. The impact of this feature on definition of such designators is considered in the next chapter.

We must now make an important observation about all ought-hiding and goal-oriented designators. In each the evaluative component is an integral part of the designator and cannot be removed without changing the overall meaning. ("Too much" will never be used seriously and literally to approve of anything; its very existence is for complaining.) For this reason we say such designators are **formal** evaluators, in contra-distinction to the environmental "Jew" and "nigger," which tomorrow may conceivably be perceived neutrally. Thus in our attempts to rewrite descriptive and evaluative components separately, we are driven to such seemingly far-fetched versions as the "Negative Income Tax" example attempted earlier. Ironically, it is these ought-hiding mixed evaluators, so difficult to detect and analyze, which trigger most communication breakdowns when men of goodwill convene to resolve differences.

Value predictions: the "ought" assertion.   What happens when, instead of hiding the ought, the producer flaunts it for all to see?

> You ought to drive more carefully.
> We should recognize Communist China.
> We must get tough—or give up!

Earlier we said such assertions were partly cognitive and partly directive—that is, the producer is trying to tell us something about the world and at the same time to get us to do something about it.

And since, as the consumer, you won't (or shouldn't!) buy the directive part without the description, you will want to pull out and examine whatever claim is being made.

Let's take the second example. What claim(s) about the world does it contain? The sentence itself tells us nothing. But behind it are certain implied **predictions** regarding recognition of Communist China (better negotiation, etc.) plus implied **approval** of these alleged results. Thus the name "value prediction"—and thus the need again to separate descriptive from evaluative components. Schematically:

> Recognizing Communist China will produce x, y, z.   **(Descriptive)**
>
> Continued non-recognition will produce (or continue)   **(Descriptive)**
>   p, q, r.
>
> x, y, z (the combination) **is better than** p, q, r.   **(Evaluative)**

(Note the virtual identity of this model with that of "progressive" given earlier.)

One may argue that we have put too many words in the producer's mouth. But there is no other way to assign to his assertion a validity which he surely expects. For the consumer may doubt his predictions OR disclaim his values. (Maybe WE like p, q, r better than x, y, z!) In short, unless the producer is willing to have his "ought" assertion weighed for both accuracy of prediction and acceptability of evaluation, we are—and should be—unwilling to pay it any attention at all.

External evaluators

As if the internal evaluators—discussed at such length in the foregoing pages—were not enough, we have developed a way of casting aspersions from the outside. **Quotation marks**—the verbal equivalent of the arched eyebrow—now settle themselves neatly around an otherwise neutral designator and disparage or defame whatever it denotes. To repeat an earlier example, if I say, "He's a northern liberal," no value component is present. But if I write, "He's one of those northern 'liberals'," I probably mean: "He calls himself 'liberal' (descriptive) but the word 'liberal' is far too good (evaluative) for what he really is." The platonic assumption here is that "liberal" has some original meaning which it is somehow wrong to change, regardless of extent of agreement. The practical assumption is that the left wing has wrested the word "liberal" from the right, who must either steal it back or divest it of its favorable aura. In any case, quotation marks used in such a manner clearly add an evaluative component to an otherwise literal assertion.

Assuming one is able to produce some completely descriptive assertions—free from evaluators of any kind—we can still tip the scale one way or another by careful selection of **sentential connectors.** A handful of logical conjunctions such as "and," "or," "implied," and "because" are capable of hitching two assertions together without favoring either. Once we stray into other connectors, however, we are almost sure to insert a value element. "But," for example, the commonest replacement for "and," usually favors its consequent over its antecedent. "Tom is faster, but Jim is a better passer," usually signifies (or defends) the coach's intention to use Jim rather than Tom. Reverse the assertions—"Jim is a better passer, but Tom is faster"— and one tends to place Tom above Jim on the momentary value-scale.

"But" evaluates more markedly in an argument: A asserts something B can't deny; so B supplies a truth of his own, preceded by ". . . That may be true, **but.** . . ." Similar evaluations are suggested by "although," "even though," and "while it is true that . . . it must also be remembered that. . . ." In each case, one person tries to assert a truth somehow more important than that of the other's. And, as noted earlier, importance is not a property of a truth or a proposition, but rather someone's evaluation of it. Thus may two descriptive assertions, conjoined by an evaluative connector, lead a consumer to favor one assertion over the other. In most cases the value elements may be removed by stating the two assertions separately or by connecting them with "and."

Unfortunately—for the consumer, at least—the evaluative conjunction is unnecessary if the truths are selected carefully. Propaganda analysts have long lamented the bland series of carefully selected descriptions—all true—which collectively praise or damn their objects as surely as all the linguistic evaluators we can find. Even single descriptions—"Uncle Al is sober tonight"—may imply enough to lead to unfavorable evaluation.[7] But such matters are clearly outside a study of value language; for the language itself is purely descriptive.

---

[7] Roland Hall, "Excluders," **Analysis,** 20 (1959), 1–7.

Final observations about value language

One must be struck by the size of the value component in our every-day language. When one removes the evaluations, the commands, the emotive ejaculations, etc., there is not much pure description left. Toulmin[8] notes that much of what we call "description" is actually definitive in function (see Chapter Six for a complete discussion of description versus definition), and Austin[9] points out that some of what we now call description (for example, "I pronounce you man and wife") is not cognitive in function at all, but rather performative or commemorative. Perhaps all this reflects an age where mass media report the world to us all at once; and soon each of us knows what the other knows. To describe to one another in such a world is largely redundant.

The form in which most mixed evaluations occur—with traditional value words such as "good," "right," and "just," conspicuous by their absence—confirms a reluctance to own up to the value components of our mixed value assertions. "Pass the salt" is the best way to get salt; why should disapproval of the skate dance be hidden in such ostensi-ble descriptions as, "that disgusting performance" or "degenerate dancing"? The traditional notion suggested earlier—that we tend to project our passions onto their objects—is perhaps an oversimplifi-cation. More probably our natural wish to clothe in respectable ob-jectivity our feelings about the world, is interwoven with our instinctive understanding that our evaluations are **not entirely** about ourselves and our descriptions **not entirely** about their object.

Finally, if you have been skeptical of the attempt to categorize the many ways in which evaluation thrusts itself into our language, allow me to add my skepticism to yours. Surely any attempt to reduce evalu-ative discourse to strict categories must contend in the end with overlap and blur. For language has a way of hewing to the needs of its users. And in the present state of human response, what we think, what we feel, what we like, what we want, and what we demand are very mixed up; our language merely reflects that mixture. If, when someone says, "That was a good book!" he is in part describing his

[8] S. E. Toulmin and H. Baier, "On Describing," **Mind,** LXI (1952), 13–38.
[9] J. L. Austin, **How To Do Things with Words: The William James Lectures De-livered at Harvard University in 1955** (Cambridge, Mass.: Harvard University Press, 1962), pp. 1–11.

standards, in part declaring that the book meets these standards, in part defending the standards, in part urging their adoption, in part expressing exuberance over a gratifying experience, in part trying not to be alone—it is because **that is the kind of being he is.**

Applications

For the extemporaneous speaker. You may well wonder, after reading this chapter, how a speaker who must choose his words on the spur of the moment can possibly keep track of all his mixed evaluative assertions. The answer is: He can't. Do not be surprised if in your next few speeches you find yourself using evaluative language much as you have in the past. Remember, even if you were able to purge your language of all evaluation, it wouldn't say what you want it to say. And besides, nobody would want to listen. The very fact that you now recognize evaluative language when you see or hear it, is laying a base that will enable you to use such language with more discretion—and with a greater sense of ethical responsibility—in your speaking in the future.

For the debater. Prepare a brief argument on a controversial subject, trying to avoid the use of any evaluative conjunctions. If you find the word "but" creeping into your discourse, ask yourself whether its omission (or replacement with "and") would affect the **logic** of your argument. If you have an opportunity to record a debate or a portion thereof, play it back and see how many evaluative conjunctions you can spot, especially in your own speaking. You will probably note many more in the rebuttal stage, as you warm to the task of making your truth seem more important than that of your opponent. And when you catch an opponent conceding one of your points and following the concession with "but," ask yourself whether his new point actually refutes or bears upon yours.

For the participant in group discussion. Tape a portion of your next discussion. Play it back at your leisure, making note of the use and abuse of evaluative language. If you find places in the discussion where the participants seem heated beyond justification, or where communication stumbles or breaks down, see if you can trace the difficulty to the use of mixed evaluative assertions by one or more participants. If you can isolate a single sentence which seems to have caused the difficulty, try to reassert the context of the sentence in more neutral language without destroying the referential intent of its producer.

Summary

Value language is that with which we express approval or disapproval. Pure value language is uncommon in everyday discourse. Mixed evaluative assertions—in which we describe and evaluate simultaneously —occur in many forms. Some of these are: subjective connotation, metaphor, hiding-the-ought, and external evaluators (quotation marks and evaluative conjunctions). Stating separately the descriptive component of a mixed evaluative assertion often helps to reveal the evaluative component.

Questions and exercises

1. On almost any of television's Western reruns you will at some time hear the villain say, "Are you threatening me?"—to which the hero will invariably reply, "No, I'm warning you." Is there any difference between a threat and a warning, other than the fact that good guys warn and bad guys threaten? To be sure of your answer, see if you can formulate the descriptive components of each of these two designators.

2. The word "quack" is a mixed evaluative designator referring to a certain kind of doctor. In the sentence, "Dr. Jones is a quack," see if you can replace "quack" with its descriptive component. As a last resort, check your dictionary.

3. Webster's Third International Dictionary defines "ants in one's pants" as "obvious and excessive eagerness for action: Restlessness, impatience." Is it possible to use this metaphor in other than a derogatory manner? Try it in some sample contexts before finalizing your answer.

4. Go through the "Get Tough" passage from Chapter One, underscoring the mixed evaluative assertions. Next, see if you can fit them into the categories given in this chapter. Finally, pick two or three and rewrite, excluding the value component. Did you include "minority axe" as an evaluative metaphor?

5. Try your hand at rewriting each of the three following reports, excluding from each the evaluative component. When you've finished, compare your rewrite of the first report with the one given below. Are there descriptive components in the original which do not show in the rewrite? If so, can you add them without inserting an evaluative component?

a. Eyebrows were raised on Capitol Hill yesterday when a special House investigating subcommittee revealed that Senator John Wilson, key member of the Senate Armed Services Committee, was a former lobbyist for an unnamed missiles company. When finally cornered by Associated Press reporters, Senator Wilson admitted he had lobbied for the company, but refused to say whether he still had "financial connections" therewith.

b. In yesterday's battle of the track and field titans, South High emerged victorious despite a lackluster performance by its highly vaunted mile-relay team. Nursing an earlier disappointing 4' 15" effort in the mile, South's Frank Johnson had a comfortable 5-yard margin when he grabbed the baton for his anchor lap in the relay. But even though running on his home track, Johnson was unable to stave off a remarkable finish by East's Paul Edwards, and South had to settle for an uncomfortable second in this key race.

c. As the nationwide steel strike enters its third week, labor representatives are still refusing to budge from their original demands. Special evaluators, called in by the employers solely to make sure labor was bargaining in good faith, had the rug pulled out from under them when an NLRB ruling banned them from the bargaining table. Thus, while a do-nothing government stands by, a handful of "Big Labor" bosses continue to penalize the consumer and throw sand in the wheels of industrial progress and harmony.

Rewrite of "a". Yesterday a special House investigating subcommittee announced that Senator John Wilson, member of the Senate Armed Services Committee, was a former lobbyist for a missiles company. When interviewed by Associated Press reporters, Senator Wilson stated that he had lobbied for the company. He did not say whether he still had financial connections therewith.

SIX

Clarifying language

So far we have assumed that language would be used to describe the world (to indicate its features and talk about them), to attempt to control this world—especially the people in it—and now and then to express how we feel about the things and people we encounter. This would be fine if every bit of discourse struck home, and there were no communication breakdowns. But you and I know that language doesn't always hit its mark. To see how easy it is to miss, we need only look again at the four-fold meaning diagram from Chapter Two. (See next page.) You may have noticed when you first saw this model that all broken lines conveniently converged on "W." That is, the piece of language used was expected to call forth for the consumer the same portion of the world that the producer had in mind. But what happens when we know—or suspect—that our contraption has misfired; that producer and consumer are not on the same wave length?

Plainly, language needs a self-correcting mechanism so that, much as a moving stream of water purifies itself, discourse may be clarified as it goes along. Unhappily such a mechanism exists only in part; and what is there is often misunderstood and abused. In this chapter we shall examine some of these explicative devices and suggest some orderly procedures for clarifying language.

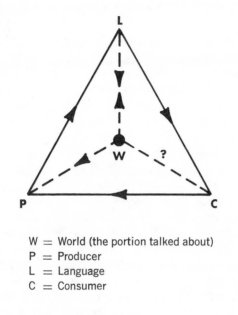

W = World (the portion talked about)
P = Producer
L = Language
C = Consumer

Using language to clarify language

Throughout this study of language we have observed that what a bit of language looks like is not so important as how it behaves in a given context. Thus it is with language used to clarify language. There is no way to tell by looking at (or listening to) a given bit of communication whether its intent is **descriptive** or **definitive**—that is, about the world or about itself.

Let's back up a bit. Suppose you are talking or writing, busily making your point (whether it be cognitive, directive, expressive, or a combination)—when you suddenly become aware that a portion of your discourse has failed to get through to your consumers. What do you do? If you are a typical communicator you will take a moment out from your objective and produce some discourse aimed at clarifying what has gone before. And while this discourse may look or sound very much like the rest, its **definitive function** makes it subject to a whole new set of rules. Thus our first task is to focus on this definitive function and to observe some of the devices used to accomplish it.

Naming and pointing. "Me Tarzan, you Jane!" Devotees of this marathon television and movie saga may have missed the original Edgar Rice Burroughs story in which Tarzan and Jane find a common language by the name-and-point method. Anyone attempting to converse with a foreigner will find this device inescapable; and strangely enough this is the principal way we enlarge vocabularies in our own language. We do not learn the meaning of "dog" by consulting a dictionary, but rather by watching men point at a dog and say "dog." This is the way babies learn what adults mean with the words they use. And it works! So why do we need anything else?

If our entire vocabulary consisted of individual designators, we could probably get on quite well with the name-and-point method. When I point to John and say "John" my meaning is unambiguous. And with a little effort we can make the system work for classes as well. If we point to enough individual chairs and say "chair," the consumer soon gets the idea. Even with classes, however, we may run afoul of ambiguity. As we point and utter "chair" the consumer may think "wood" or "sit." Viewers of Walt Disney's **Bambi** were delighted as the fawn was taught "flower" by being shown a field of flowers. When a skunk popped his head up in the middle the fawn promptly named him "flower." Here the concept that came across was not "pretty with petals on a stem" but "anything in this field."

With considerably more effort, the name-and-point method can be made to work for property designators. If we point at enough blue items, taking care that they have nothing in common except blueness, our consumer will soon eliminate from his thinking possible individuals and classes, and will fix upon the property called "blue." Designators of simple properties such as "is running" are harder to fix on by naming and pointing, but quite easy to demonstrate.

When we come to relation designators, however, our system falls flat. Suppose someone says, "Communists have taken hold of our government." Assume for the moment that we are satisfied with "communists" and "government," but we wonder what is meant by "has taken hold of." Even assuming the producer knows what he means, what can he point to that will help us understand him? Grabbing hold of some physical object won't help, since this is a metaphorical relation. (It is impossible physically to take hold of a government.) Except for the simplest spacial concepts, name-and-point is of little use in clarifying relation designators, and other methods must be sought.

Drawing and demonstrating. When a bit of language is not clear, and its object is not handy, we often draw pictures. When used in this manner the picture is a visual substitution for a written or spoken word. But while just about anything can be named, only certain things can be literally depicted by a drawing. So the picture is of limited value in clarifying language.

The half-brother of the picture is the demonstration. If I want to make the word "glissading" clear to a consumer, and there is some snow handy, my best bet is probably a quick demonstration. Like the picture, the demonstration is useful only for certain types of designators. Using pictures and demonstrations to clarify **language** is only a hair away from the use of visual aids to clarify **ideas**—a process familiar to all speakers.

Using the language. When we said that babies learn by watching adults name and point, we told only part of the story. Much linguistic learning occurs by watching language in action—by looking or listening while an unfamiliar designator is used by sophisticated users in a variety of ways. If the surrounding language is familiar enough the consumer will soon narrow down and isolate the meaning of the new word. (This method of tying new language to the world is popular among college students who, preferring to keep hidden the narrow limits of their vocabularies, listen to a lecture with a look of fixed wisdom, behind which the wheels race madly trying to fit the unfamiliar words into place.) Capitalizing on the typical consumer's willingness to play this guessing game, producers shy unwisely away from other clarifying devices, saying to themselves in effect: "After I've used this word a few times they'll get the hang of it."

Coffee-pot. What do you do if you are listening to a speech, and you are suddenly struck with the word "porturate"? Not having a dictionary handy you start by making some guesses. First the "-ate" at the end suggests a verb or an adjective—in either case, some kind of property designator. Quickly you settle for the verb (he said "por-tur-**ate**," not "por-tur-**uht**")—and all the while you listen as the producer uses the word:

> One often porturates after a brisk swim. (Physical? Mental?)
>
> It's fun to lie in the sun and porturate. (Enjoyable—probably mental)
>
> When viewing suddenly a field of wildflowers, I cannot resist taking a deep breath and porturating. (Exultation?)
>
> We stood silently in a moment of sheer porturation.

(Now I think I get it—"porturate" refers to that half-grateful, half-exuberant reveling in the sheer joy of being alive!)

The careful reader may have noticed a similarity between the above exercise and the parlor game "coffee-pot." The game is normally played by sending one person from the room while the rest fix on some intransitive verb. When the "it" returns, he asks a series of yes-or-no questions, using (for some strange reason) the phrase "coffee-pot" to replace the unknown verb. "Can one coffee-pot in the morning?" "Does coffee-potting take place indoors?" This continues until the guesser is able to discover the chosen verb.

Looking back at the "porturate" exercise, we see the coffee-potting process at work. Instead of the question used in the game, however, we have statements—apparently referential statements. But there is a crucial difference between these four assertions and referential statements which aim to describe the world. For these assertions were aimed not at describing something but rather at clarifying a common designator.

This coffee-potting process—using a descriptive form to accomplish a definitive function—is another example of language looking like one thing and acting like another. So closely welded is this hybrid form that it may be difficult to recognize even in your own discourse, let alone in that of anyone else. Two features should tip you off that the producer may be coffee-potting:

1. When several sentences in a row contain the same unfamiliar designator, their function is probably (in part at least) that of clarifying language.

2. The pseudo-statements used in this language-clarifying device do not call for verification. It makes no sense to question or deny "One often porturates after a brisk swim." One must **assume** that the producer is telling the truth before one can gain a better understanding of "porturate." This latter clue is a matter of sensitive guessing, and points up the potential danger in the entire process. For it is a small step from innocuous coffee-potting to the fallacious use of a single sentence to define and describe—a matter discussed in a later section.

We have casually referred to all these clarifying devices as definitive in function, suggesting perhaps that they are different kinds of definition. But it should be noted that naming and pointing, demonstrating, pictures, and even coffee-potting are all ways of **suggesting** a connection between a word and the world. Definition—a process of offering alternative language—is something else. And so great are the misconceptions which have plagued definition over the centuries that the remainder of this chapter will be devoted to consideration of the nature and types of definition.

Definition as a clarifier of language

Starting with the approximate notion that definition is a process of language substitution for purposes of clarity, let us attend to some of the misconceptions and confusions that seem to beset this process.

Misconceptions about definition.
1. That definition can tell us the essence of things.

Having observed that designators may be meaningful in any of several ways, we should not be surprised to learn that "definition" itself has many distinct meanings. One popular distinction is that of **nominal** definitions, which are said to be about language, and **real** definitions, said to be about things. We shall hold ultimately that definition is a linguistic process; so it will behoove us to examine closely the process called "real definition" to see exactly what is taking place.

A scientist isolates a new metal and calls it "luminum." He describes its properties, and his colleagues hail the definition of a new metal. But what actually happened?

> A new metal was isolated. (That is a physical process, and we can find little reason to call this process "definition.")
>
> The scientist named the substance and made notes (to himself) about it.
>
> The scientist secured his colleagues' (and ultimately, the English-speaking world's) tacit acceptance of the symbolic connection between "luminum" and the newly-found substance.

This last process comes close to what we shall mean by "definition"—but note that there is nothing **real** about the process; it is purely **nominal** (linguistic) activity. Thus we must conclude that what is called "real definition" is partly a physical process (not a definition at all) and partly a disguised nominal definition; and definition is not about things but about their names—about language.

You may require a minute or two to see how the verbal part of this definitive process tells us nothing about the world. It may help to assume the same situation—the discovery of luminum—with one exception: the scientist is a fraud. When one performs the operation indicated in his definition one gets, not a new metal, but nothing. What impact does this unexpected state of affairs have on the definition of "luminum"? **None whatever!** The designator still means exactly what it meant in the first place—only the thing to which it refers doesn't exist. That is, the designator now joins "unicorn" and "the present King of Mexico" as a partial designator—having connotation but no denotation.[1] Thus if "luminum" is any criterion, definitions are not real but nominal—not about things but about their names.

2. **That dictionary definitions relate words to the world.**

Closely related to the "real-nominal" confusion is the notion that dictionaries somehow tie the words we don't know to the things they stand for. A moment's reflection will reveal what a strange notion this is. Open any dictionary and, to the right of the word to be defined, you will find not cats, dogs, and people, but more words. The writer of the dictionary cannot pin the world to its pages. He can only offer more words, with the hope that these are more helpful than the word you looked up. Again, definition operates within language. To tie a piece of language to the part of the world it names, other devices must be used.

3. **That there are true and false definitions.**

Students (and professors!) of public speaking are often puzzled or angered when they open a dictionary to "extemporaneous" and find, listed as a synonym, "impromptu." Extemporaneous and impromptu are not the same, they say, and to define one as synonymous with the other is to produce a false definition. Again, a moment's thought will show that there is something wrong with the use of the word "false" here. You were warned earlier of the erroneous assumption that every designator has a necessary tie to its object. And yet there is surely something wrong (if not false) in listing "extemporaneous" and "impromptu" as synonyms. In order to resolve this problem we will have

[1] Mathematicians define "the square root of minus one" as that number which, multiplied by itself, results in minus one. The fact that there is no such number does not bother them in the least. An entire sub-system of imaginary numbers—yielding important consequences for the physicist as well as the mathematician—is based on this carefully defined (partial) designator.

to make an important distinction—that of reported and stipulated definitions.

A **reported definition** is a linguistic equivalent stated by a dictionary (or some other authority) based on the way people talk. If in the past you have regarded the dictionary as some kind of oracle, you may be disappointed to learn it can do naught but report. True, the dictionary may report the language habits of whatever portion of society its authors choose; and often there is talk about correct and incorrect usage. But the real choice in this matter is not theirs but ours. In general, the report reflects the speaking and writing of whomever you and I choose to emulate.

A **stipulated definition** says that a given piece of language will be used in a certain way, with the stipulator promising to abide by the agreement. It should be noted immediately that this process occurs entirely within language. Thus the producer, in giving us some alternate language in case the first bit didn't work, is telling us that we're free to make the substitution anywhere in his discourse—for whatever good it may do us.

An obvious question: Why stipulate? Why not use the definition the dictionary reports to us? There are many reasons why you, as a producer of discourse, may find it advantageous to stipulate a definition. A dictionary may present several closely related choices, thus requiring a stipulation as to which one is intended. Some words are habitually used with such vague and shifting meaning that a precise stipulation is required. Sometimes the producer is coining a new word or giving an old word a new twist. But most important is that feature noted briefly in Chapter Four: that those designators most often requiring definition are comprised not of one word but of many. Because the permutation of word combinations soon becomes astronomical the dictionary is compelled to report words to us one at a time, with occasional sojourns into two-word and three-word combinations. Where in the dictionary would you find "those who are bent on destroying our country by senseless rioting"? If this complex designator is ever to be defined, it will be by stipulation—not by report.

Now that we have made a distinction between reported and stipulated definitions, we can get back to that matter of whether definitions themselves can be true or false. Let's take a reported definition first.

> Fox: any of certain carnivorous fur-bearing animals, smaller than wolves, and noted for their craftiness.

Clearly what is true here is not the definition but the **report** of the definition. Men either do or do not use the word "fox" to refer to such animals. Viewed in this light a dictionary serves as a kind of current history book, reporting to us the language habits of the English-speaking community. Thus its **reports** are certainly true or false. The **definitions** themselves are not.

Stipulated definitions are equally incapable of truth or falsity, but for another reason. When I say, "I shall use the term 'Negative Income Tax' to mean . . . ," I have stipulated a definition of "Negative Income Tax." In one sense I am declaring my intentions to use this bit of language in a certain way. In another sense I am directing my consumers to perceive the designator in this way if they wish to understand me. In the first sense—unless you make the absurd assumption that I am lying about my intentions—we can no more call the stipulation "false" than we could deny the minister's "I now pronounce you man and wife." In the second sense, as a kind of instruction to the consumer, my stipulation is a command. And, as Black suggests, "to call it false would be as absurd as to call 'let's go for a walk' a lie."[2]

One wonders whether this laborious investigation into the truth properties of definition has been worth the trouble. But it will soon become extremely important to distinguish definition from description. And as they both look so much alike structurally—in our discourse as well as that of others—we shall be driven to ask whether any real claim about the world is being made. Descriptions make such claims; definitions do not.

4. That only class designators need defining.

A dictionary is equally friendly toward class, individual, property, and relation designators. It will define any of them for you. But outside the dictionary, definition seems inevitably—and strangely—confined to class designators. Any formal instruction you may have had in the art of defining probably exemplified with designators of classes. If in a speech you find yourself saying, "We should (or should not) have a Negative Income Tax," you will be quick to offer a definition of "Negative Income Tax"; but you would never think to define "should."[3] And if a speaker asserts to his audience, "Medicare costs too much,"

[2] Max Black, **Critical Thinking: An Introduction to Logic and Scientific Method** (New York: Prentice-Hall, Inc., 1946), p. 190.
[3] Debaters often define "should" as "ought to, but not necessarily will." This helps little, merely transferring the unknown from "should" to "ought." See Chapter Five for a complete analysis of "should."

there will be ten listeners who will ask themselves "What does he mean by 'Medicare'?" for every one who wonders what the speaker means by "too much." And yet we saw in Chapter Five how troublesome were "should" and "too much," and how they thrust an evaluative component into any sentence in which they appear. Later, when we examine some popular methods for defining, we shall find them remarkably tailor-made for names of classes.

5. **That definition is a matter of defining single words.**

In an earlier discussion on stipulated definition we noted the futility of searching in the dictionary for "those who are bent on destroying our country by senseless rioting." In fact, the dictionary will be of no help at all in determining the meaning of this eleven-word designator. Even hunting up the definition of each word separately doesn't help us much in putting the parts together in the way the author intended. This fact should alert us to the danger of using complex designators of this sort without definition—unless, of course, we are deliberately trying to confuse the consumer.

The same is true of the designator, "Negative Income Tax." If you were to find yourself using this three-word phrase in a communication situation where it might be misunderstood, and you decided to offer a definition, you might be tempted to define "negative" and "income" and "tax" separately. But this would give your consumer little hint of the overall meaning. Thus the need to distinguish and define designators rather than words—that is, to be able to separate discourse into its **indicators,** which name what we speak of, and the **predicators,** with which we say things about them.

The actual nature of definition. If all these are misconceptions about definition, what is the truth about the process? What is definition and what does it do?

Viewed in its simplest aspect, a definition is little more than a verbal equivalence attached to a permission slip. The verbal equivalence tells us what language we may substitute for the language being defined. The permission slip assures us that we may make the substitution anywhere in a given body of discourse.[4] This is a bold promise by the producer; and we must grant him two general exceptions:

1. No matter how sure one is of one's definition, it is never permissible to substitute in quoted discourse. The quotation marks en-

---

[4] This last criterion is sometimes called the "principle of universal substitution."

close the exact words somebody used. If we change a single word, the parent statement is no longer true. For example, assume "man" is defined as "rational animal":

> John said, "Here comes a man." (True)
> John said, "Here comes a rational animal." (False)

Philosophers sometimes call such a situation an **oblique context.** Among other forms are: "John believes," "John understands," "John feels." Definitive substitutions in the noun clauses following such phrases may well render a true statement false.

2. If I should speak of an Officer's Mess, and you were to replace "mess" with its familiar definitive equivalent "confusion," the result would be "an officer's confusion"—not at all what I started with. And it would do you no good to wave a dictionary in my face. The mess I was talking about is an eating place, something quite different from your use of "mess." The point is that, while "mess" is one word, it is many designators—as many as there are meanings for it. The problem, then, is one of **multiple designation**—another situation where definitive substitution will not work. As with oblique context, multiple designation should cause little trouble provided one stays alert to what is going on.

Viewed as an operation (as opposed to a product of that operation) definition **is the process of offering replacement for a designator and authorizing universal substitution of the replacement in a given body of discourse.** Thus the uniqueness of the defining process: It does not name-and-point, nor draw pictures, nor use the language in question. Instead it offers us **more language** which purports to be more helpful in some way than the original. And since it is the producer who is primarily responsible for the clarity of his discourse, we shall look at definition first from his viewpoint, asking in turn the three questions he must ask himself: When to define. Where to define. How to define.

When to define. The producer defines (offers substitute language for) a designator when he has reason to believe the original language will go awry. A reaction by the consumer—or knowledge of the average consumer's language—tells the producer his communication effort will probably fail. This failure of producer and consumer to converge on the same piece of the world may happen in either of two ways. To understand exactly how these two breakdowns occur, we must look

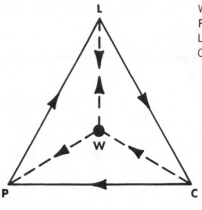

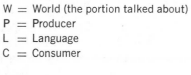

W = World (the portion talked about)
P = Producer
L = Language
C = Consumer

Figure A

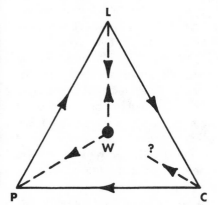

Figure B

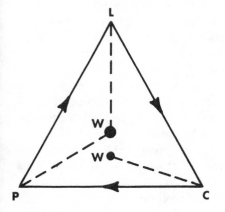

Figure C

once again at the Meaning Diagram from Chapter Two, this time with some variations. (See preceding page.)

Figure A shows linguistic meaning when it works. The consumer is familiar not only with the language being used but also with the portion of the world referred to; and he has earlier established a connection between the two, so that the production of L calls forth W. In Figure B we see that something is missing. The consumer has perceived the language but (whether or not he has heard it before) he is unable to connect it to anything in the world.

Figure C presents a different—and much more dangerous—problem. Here the consumer has made a connection between the producer's language and the world—but it's the wrong part of the world! The danger here is that the consumer will continue listening or reading, certain that he is on the beam. And by the time the breakdown is discovered much damage has been done, and misunderstandings have to be corrected. During World War II, many Britons characterized American battle efforts as "putting on a good show." It took us a while to learn that "putting on a good show" designated a noble effort, not a theatrical attempt to grab headlines. Similar examples can be cited from modern attempts at international communication, and are not unheard of in family political discussions across the breakfast table.

Let us assume that you as producer have determined that one of these two breakdown conditions is present. One of your designators is not ringing a bell; thus a definition is called for. But (to be blunt about it) you are right in the middle of some rather poignant rhetoric; and you hate to interrupt it for something as earthy as a definition. Where can you crank in some substitute language so it can do its job, and at the same time interfere least with the flow of communication? This is a matter, not of when to define, but of where in one's discourse a definition should go.

Where to define.   In actual practice we are likely to find definitions almost anywhere. A producer will unburden himself of a seven-syllable word, and then, realizing that he has almost no chance of being understood, belatedly offer a definition—usually in the sentence following the one with the word in question.

This practice of mixing our definitions right in with the rest of the discourse has two drawbacks which, between them, should lead us to seek a better way.

1. When we mix definitions and descriptions in the same paragraph

it is often difficult to tell them apart. If in the middle of a discourse on socialism I say, "Socialism is enlightened capitalism," am I defining "socialism" or describing how socialism works in the world? It would be fine if we could speak our definitions in a tone different from that we use for the rest of our discourse or, when writing, put the communication itself on the right side of the page and the clarifying definitions on the left. But in fact we do neither; and the consumer is often left guessing. Later we shall see the importance of keeping definition and description separate in our thinking if not in our speaking and writing.

2. The place we choose for definition in our discourse may have a marked effect on how it is accepted. As a producer of informative discourse you will on occasion find it necessary to use a long, pretentious-sounding designator which may well throw your consumer into a state of shock. Unless this is your intent (and we hope it isn't!) you will want some way to ease the pain. And yet, if you are a typical informative speaker you will go right ahead and use the word. Then, having inadvertently dropped a psychological barrier between you and your consumer, you will belatedly offer a definition and tell yourself that everything is now all right. Do this two or three times in the space of a few minutes, and you will probably notice your listener showing signs of battle fatigue. While this consumer resistance to strange language is problem enough for the writer, it may be crucial for the speaker, whose consumers have little chance to take notes and no chance to use a dictionary.

What can a producer do to minimize the impact of strange words? Assume for the moment that you are trying to explain to an audience how the volume control on a radio works. If you follow your instincts you will probably come up with something like this: "The volume level in your set is controlled by a rheostat" (blank looks from your consumers). "Well, a rheostat is an adjustable resistor" (more blank looks). "Sometimes they call them potentiometers" (worse than ever!). "Anyway, the rheostat operates on . . ."

By this time your consumers, while possibly impressed with your vocabulary, are quite probably dazed or even offended. An after-test would probably show that very little of your informative communication got through. Now let's try it another way.

"Some of the earliest table-model radios had two volume levels: too soft and too loud. If you wanted to listen comfortably you had to change your seat. Something was needed to enable the user to adjust the volume to his own need. Modern radios have a device which does this job: It's called a rheostat. You simply turn the volume knob . . . "

Many errors of definition have been corrected in the second version. The point to remember here is the **location** of the definition and of the designator being defined. First a need was created, then a definition of "rheostat" was introduced **as a solution to the need.** Only after the consumer had been thus prepared for the new designator was "rheostat" actually introduced.

How to define.   Almost any book on semantics or critical thinking will include a section entitled "Methods of Definition." One popular work lists twenty-five different ways to define. Others vary in the number of methods offered, with the average running around six or seven. This wide disparity should suggest an obvious truth: There is no more a set number of methods of definition than there is a finite number of ways to compose a speech or write a poem. Most of the recommended ways of defining can be reduced to three simple processes. As we examine these three methods, see if you notice a peculiar limitation exhibited by each.

1. **Definition by genus-and-difference.** Capitalizing on a highly refined system of empirical classification present in most cultures, definition by genus-and-difference works as follows: Identify the object of the designator to be defined by naming its parent family or order— its **genus.** (For instance, a pencil belongs to the family of writing instruments, an orange to the family of fruit.) Next, name the properties which distinguish the object from other members of its family— the **difference.** When you have named these two aspects of an object you have defined its designator. Thus "man is a rational animal," offers a definition in which "animal" names the general class to which man belongs and "rational" the property which distinguishes him from other animals.[5] This is by far the most popular way to define, partly because it is traditional and partly because it works. It works because most people tend to **think** in systems of classification, and are quick to find a pigeon-hole for something new.

Now is the time to reexamine some of those formal evaluators that caused so much trouble in Chapter Five. Remember "progress"? We said progress is a kind of change, but all change is not progress. Restated in genus-and-difference language, the genus of progress is

---

[5] We ought in fact to say, "Man is an animal rational," naming the genus first. This is proper syntax in many languages.

change. But what can we list as the difference? The difference (between progress and other kinds of change) must lie in the goal or direction by which the change is measured. But what happens if you and I don't like the implied goal or direction? If half the meaning of "progress"—its difference—is not acceptable for all consumers, can this word be used meaningfully?

Designators like "progress" whose only difference is evaluative are clearly dangerous, and must be produced and consumed with utmost caution. Each user of the language must be allowed to retain his own values. Indiscriminate use of formal evaluators can tend to steal away this right through the fear of being labeled "against progress." The impact of evaluative difference may be seen in the following diagram:

EVALUATIVE DIFFERENCE

GENUS:	CHANGE (Movement)	Appropriate Designator:
		"progress"
	DIFFERENCE: Favorable	"improvement"
		"advancement"
		"elevation"
		"deterioration"
	DIFFERENCE: Unfavorable	"retrogression"
		"degeneration"
		"distortion"
	DIFFERENCE: Contrary to expectation	"perversion"

Note that each of the designators in the right-hand column means nothing more than "change" or "movement," except in terms of what is acceptable or expected.[6] Abstract classes and properties are ad-

[6] It is true that many of these words may be used neutrally; e.g., "He made progress through the snow," which may be said indiscriminately of a hero or a villain. But here the movement is measured against a stated obstacle—quite a different matter from attributing progress to a social or political change.

mittedly hard to define. But the difficulty often stems from the fact that the abstraction differs from similar notions only in terms of what we want or expect.

2. **Definition by comprehension.** Sometimes in attempting to define by genus-and-difference we find that reference to a genus is misleading or awkward or, in some cases, impossible. For example, if somebody who doesn't know baseball asks, "What is an out?" we are hardput to find the genus. Surely we are better off to reply "An out is three strikes on the batter OR a fly caught by a member of the opposing team OR . . . "—and proceed to list all the ways an out may be accomplished. If you prefer bridge to baseball, the designator "control" refers to the ability to take the first trick in a given suit. But we can hardly refer to a control as "an ability." We are much more accurate to define "control" as "either an ace or a void." These are examples of definition by comprehension; and the key feature is noted in the word "comprehension": The definitions must comprehend **all** the sub-classes. Naming just some of the sub-classes (often called "definition by example"), while frequently helpful, is not completely definitive.

Definition by comprehension is not confined to sports and games. In the National Labor Relations Acts of 1935 (Wagner Act) one finds eight activities listed under "Unfair Labor Practices." These eight activities comprise a **comprehensive definition** of "Unfair Labor Practice." One sees immediately the importance of listing all eight practices. While one might get the general idea after reading four such practices, one could conceivably engage in the other four with impunity if all eight were not listed. Should lawmakers later decide that other practices need to be added, or perhaps some deleted, appropriate adjustments can be made in the comprehensive definition.

3. **Definition by negation.** Frequently the easiest way to indicate the scope of a designator is to show what it does not designate. Thus a constitutional definition of "states' rights" might be "all powers not specifically delegated to the Federal Government." As these latter powers are presumably defined (comprehensively) in the Constitution itself, states' rights must include everything else. Note that the genus (designated here by "powers") may be stated; but instead of a difference we have a negation (exclusion) of all members of the genus except those we wish to designate. When we define "peace" as the absence of armed conflict, we don't even attempt to indicate the genus. "Peace" in this definition becomes "any state of affairs

(genus?) from which armed conflict (relatively easy to define) is absent."

Having seen three methods of definition, were you able to spot a common feature? Each of these methods is good for defining **class designators only.** The apparent reluctance of the experts to give us methods for defining other designators (e.g., property and relation) points up a fallacious assumption noted earlier, that it is class names that cause all the trouble. When in a speech on farm economics you find yourself saying, "Lowering price supports will ruin the American farmer," you may be quick to define "price supports" and even "American farmer." But you will be tempted to slide blandly over the relation designator "will ruin." And if you are inclined to say, "Well, everybody knows what 'ruin' means," compare this designator with the nine variants of "change" given in the Evaluative Difference diagram.

Definition and description

Earlier we were unhappy because definition and description, with totally different functions, look and sound exactly alike in most discourse. When in the midst of a political discussion someone says, "Socialism is enlightened capitalism," is he equating two forms of government (description) or telling us how he plans to use a certain bit of language (definition)? This is a most difficult problem in language analysis; for the producer himself may not know whether he is describing or defining. He may indeed insist upon his right to do both at the same time. And we saw in the "porturate" example near the beginning of this chapter how one may utter a series of seeming descriptions for the purpose of clarifying a common designator. But attempts to define and describe in the same sentence—as in "Socialism is enlightened capitalism"—are fraught with danger. At best the producer is confused as to the purpose of his own utterance. At worst he seeks to get his consumers' unquestioning acceptance of a doubtful description by mixing it with a seemingly harmless stipulated definition. Such hybrids of description and definition, then, try to tell us what to think before we start thinking.

Definition by the consumer

In all this discussion of definition we have assumed it was the producer who did the defining. After all, it is his discourse; he should be responsible for clarification when and where needed. But as we saw in the meaning diagram earlier in this chapter the producer has to guess when his discourse may not get through. And though a skilled communicator can guess better than a novice, he will surely on occasion let some unclear language slip through, just as now and then he will offer a laborious definition of language which was perfectly clear in the first place. When unclear discourse reaches us, we as consumers must take over the burden of definition.

How can this be done? If we don't know what he meant by that puzzling designator, how can we define it?

Drop for a moment your role as producer and assume you are consuming discourse containing one or more meaningless (to you) designators. Your first job is to study the context for clues to the missing piece. (This is of course easier with written than oral discourse. The reader has time to study the surrounding context; the listener doesn't.) The next step is to choose substitute language for the puzzling designator, saying to yourself, "I wonder if this is what he meant." Finally, make the substitution wherever the original occurs, checking to see whether the change results in any statements which are obviously false, as well as whether the overall discourse seems to make sense with the new language. You may have to repeat this process several times before you arrive at a satisfactory replacement.

Clearly this is a tall order for the consumer of discourse. If you go through this process every time some unclear language comes your way, you are likely to miss a lot of what is being said. But this fact merely underscores the urgent need for the speaker to be clear in the first place.

Note how, in their joint attempts to clarify language passing between them, producer and consumer each have certain pieces of the puzzle. Each designator the producer uses has a **comprehension probability** (C.P.) for a given consumer or consumer group. In most cases the producer is reasonably certain that his language will be clear. But definition is contemplated mostly in those uncertain cases where language may or may not get through. Here the producer has to guess whether to define or not to define. He has the same problems with his substitute language. He may in fact end up replacing what was relatively clear with something totally unintelligible. What he does (or should) know is that the substitute is a reasonably accurate replacement for the original—assuming he knows what he meant in the first place.

	C.P. (Original Language)	Accuracy of Substitution	C.P. (Substitute Language)
PRODUCER	U	K	U
CONSUMER	K	U	K

K = Known
U = Unknown
C.P. = Comprehension Probability

If the producer has failed to define where he should, the consumer has a different problem. He knows that a certain bit of language is not clear to him, otherwise he wouldn't be bothering with it. And surely he knows the meaning of his own tentative replacement language. But he doesn't know whether his replacement is what the producer intended—thus the trial-and-error process indicated above.

The bland use of the absolutes "known" and "unknown" should leave you a bit uneasy. In fact our entire approach has a yes-or-no tone which seems not to jibe with the way discourse is actually produced or consumed. This is because unclear language cannot be detected, replaced, and corrected like a defective television tube. Clarity in language is usually a matter of **degree.** Definition (or some other clarifying device) often serves, not to make unclear language clear, but to make not-so-clear language clearer. And while you have been urged throughout this chapter to keep the descriptive and definitive functions separate, your communicators will probably continue to mix them together. But understanding the two functions—as you do now —should help you both as producer and consumer in the sensitive, self-corrective, and endless task of clarifying language.

Application: rules for successful definition

The potential need for language clarification is present whenever you speak or write. And since part of the art of definition consists in knowing when to define, potential application of definitive principle must be a constant concomitant of the production of discourse. Here are some rules to help you:

For the producer

1. **Avoid using language with low comprehension probability.** If you anticipate that a certain designator will cause meaning problems for your consumer, and the designator is not crucial to your discourse, don't use it.

2. When possible, **anticipate communication misfire.**

3. When it becomes necessary to introduce a new term:
   a. **Show the need for the new concept.**
   b. **Give the replacement (familiar) language first;**
   c. Finally, **introduce the designator itself.**

4. Replace **entire designators,** not just individual words.

5. Remember the requirement of **universal substitution.** Your replacement must work anywhere the original designator appears.

6. **Do not try to define and describe in the same sentence.** Like roads and bridges, sentences have limits; it is not wise to overload them.

7. Remember to choose substitute language which you believe will **best enable the consumer to fix upon that portion of the world you wish to talk about.** Such practices as replacing a designator with language containing the original (usually called "circular definition") should be avoided, not because there is a rule against them but because they aren't likely to help the consumer. If that rare occasion should arise when a circular definition seems best, by all means use it. The ultimate test is not, does it fit technical requirements, but rather, does it work?

For the consumer.

1. **Consume discourse sympathetically.** Remember that, barring occasional chicanery, the producer is as anxious as you are for his language to get across. Careful scrutiny on your part may often reveal what he is driving at.

2. **Allow for shift in meaning.** Although we have sanctimoniously stipulated that the meaning of a designator shall not change as the discourse progresses, many producers will inadvertently or deliberately do just that—change the meaning. Careful study will often enable you to spot such a shift and facilitate detection of logical fallacy as well as semantic fallacy.

3. In trying out your hypothetical substitution, **replace the entire designator,** not individual words.

4. When your attempted replacement proves an obvious failure, **be willing to try again.** Remember: In the constant mutual attempt to bring producer and consumer together you must often do more than your share. But you will find it well worth the effort once the magic connection is made.

Summary

Language is clarified in many ways; definition is only one of these. Part of the art of producing a successful definition lies in knowing when, where, and how to define. Property and relation predicators, in addition to the obvious class indicators, often require definition. There are as many methods of definition as there are imaginative producers of discourse. Though definition and description are often attempted together, the definitive and descriptive functions are separate and distinct. The ultimate test for a definition—or for any other attempt to clarify language—lies in whether it helps the consumer relate to the world the producer has in mind.

Questions and exercises

1. The assertion "socialism is enlightened capitalism" may be a definition, a tautology or a description, depending on what assumptions we make ahead of time. What kind of assertion is it if (a) "enlightened capitalism" is assumed to be meaningful to the consumer, while "socialism" is not? (b) "socialism" has already been defined as meaning "enlightened capitalism"? (c) "socialism" and "enlightened capitalism" have each been defined independently?

2. Have you played the game "Password?" This game is played between two competing teams of two persons each. A fifth person (the referee) whispers a word to one member of each team. These members then alternate giving one-word clues to their respective partners, each trying to get his own partner to say the mystery word. When one team succeeds, a new word is supplied and the process is repeated. After you have played a few games with friends, ask yourself how the process relates to methods of definition. Does the genus-and-difference method work well or badly? Why?

3. Here is one for you mathematicians. If the dictionary had to supply definitions for all designators up to and including four-word combinations,

how many entries would be required? (Assume a million single words as a base.)

4. Reread the section entitled **"Where to Define."** Prepare a one-minute speech designed to acquaint an audience with the operation of a **hydraulic pump.** You may need a dictionary or encyclopedia to get you started. Base your speech on the unlikely assumption that your audience has never heard the phrase.

5. From the "Get Tough" passage in Chapter One, pick three designators which you feel will require defining. Stipulate a definition for each. Now go back and substitute your replacements in the original passage. Is the new version clear to you? If not, what went wrong?

6. Con you devise a defining method, comparable to genus-and-difference, comprehension or negation, for relation designators? What makes this task so difficult?

Conclusion

SOME FINAL THOUGHTS ABOUT LANGUAGE

If you have lost patience with our seemingly endless dissection process, perhaps you will be happier as we draw back and look once more at the whole. Has an overall pattern begun to appear to you? At the very least, the following generalizations should have emerged:

Doubts about meaning are often caused by failure to recognize that **language may be meaningful in many ways.**

The key to a piece of language is often not the way it looks (its form) but **how it behaves in context** (its function).

Though language is about the world, **many of its separate parts can by themselves designate nothing.**

Naming a thing doesn't guarantee the appearance of that thing in the world.

Many words may be required to indicate a **single feature** of the world.

Though we might like **dictionaries** to tie language to the world, they in fact **offer only more language.**

When language reaches us with **many functions** (e.g., descriptive, evaluative, definitive) **wrapped up in one assertion,** it is possible—and often helpful—to **extract the descriptive component** (if there is any) and **state it separately.**

But, learning all these things about our language hasn't made it (or us) any different. Our communicators, unimpressed with our discoveries, continue to talk and write in mixed-together packages like the "Get Tough" passage in Chapter One. Perhaps the best way to see how far we've come is to rewrite this passage in purely descriptive form, with all non-descriptive aspects removed or set aside.

Original

GET TOUGH—OR GIVE UP!

America is coming to a crossroads. Those who are bent on destroying our country by senseless rioting, looting, and vandalism have forced us to a point where we must protect what is left. The minority menace, forsaking the system which gave them freedom, has challenged the very roots of democracy. Can we afford to ignore this challenge?

Where is the justice in the minority axe? Where is the justice in "give-us-what-we-want-or-else"?

Of course minorities have their grievances, and these must be expressed —but only at the ballot-box! This is what democracy means. It means minorities convincing majorities that they are wrong. It means qualifying for jobs—not demanding them. It means earning the right to respectable housing, and learning to keep it respectable—not interfering with our God-given right to choose our own neighbors!

Surely the Great Creator, in blessing this land above all others, did not intend it to fall before the looter's larrup or the blackguard's blackjack. Law and order made this nation—let us not abandon it to a handful of thugs.

But even as the "liberals" stand by and cheer, the thugs are getting tough. We too must get tough—or give up!

Descriptive Rewrite

GET TOUGH—OR GIVE UP!

The people of the United States (and/or its government) are approaching a point in time where a choice is required. There is a group whose members are committed to the (physical? political?) destruction of our country by rioting, looting, and vandalism judged senseless by the author. Actions of the members of this group require that (as an alternative to acceptance of the projected destruction) we act to protect that portion of our country which may remain. There is a (black?) minority which we have reason to fear. This minority has rejected the existing government. The existing government gave the members of this minority their freedom. Actions of the minority members are in conflict with, and are (deliberately or inadvertently) likely to destroy, democratic processes. We cannot ignore this challenge without losing something we value.

There is no justice in minority violence. There is no justice in a minority position which promises violence as an alternative to stipulated actions by the majority.

It is true that minorities experience conditions to which they may legitimately object. These objections must[1] be articulated only through voting. This (voting process) is what democracy means. Democracy means members of minorities convincing majority members that the latter are wrong. Democracy means people qualifying for jobs rather than acquiring them by promising or suggesting alternatives unacceptable to us. There is an earnable right to housing respected by its occupants; democracy means not (does not mean?) altering that right.

There is a Creator who is great and who has blessed the United States more than the other nations of the world. This Creator did (does) not intend that the United States should be destroyed by violence. This nation was founded on principles of law and order. Let us not give control of it to a number (considered small) of violence-oriented activists.

While those who call themselves "liberal" observe and express approval, these activists are predicting and implying, as alternatives to whatever they seek, actions unacceptable to us. We must propose and enforce alternatives equally unacceptable to them, or give to these activists such control of the nation as we now hold.

The first thing one notices is that the rewrite is rather longer than the original. Apparently referential precision—if that's what the rewrite is—comes only with lengthy, awkward, even painful construction. Surely nobody would point to such discourse as a model of spoken or written elegance! And if the pure description is in some way a component of the original, how can a part be larger than the whole? Presumably while reducing ambiguity and uncertainty we have increased the verbal machinery! Much as a car driver shifting gears for a hill gains power at the expense of speed, linguistic assertion seems capable of economy or referential precision—but not both at the same time.

Next, when we try to trace the steps by which we got from the first

---

[1] To save space, value predictions like "must" will remain unchanged. Full analysis would require separation into predictive and evaluative components (see Chapter Five).

version to the second, we come up with quite a list. Non-referential language with obvious cognitive intent has been rewritten in referential form. Questions and commands which hid assertions now appear as statements. Syntactical ambiguities have been clarified. Hidden evaluators have been rooted out, leaving bare description. Definitive substitutions for vague designators have rendered the parent statements more readily verifiable. We have, in short, applied to the "Get Tough" original most of the theory of the preceding chapters.

Finally, we must disavow any implied equivalence of the two versions. The original is filled with metaphors, questions, evaluations, and partial designations because it reflects what its author feels and thinks and believes as well as what he sees. It is important that we be able to state the descriptive portion of such discourse; for only this portion is capable of truth. But truth is not the only value in discourse; and the non-descriptive components may on occasion comprise the only real significance. The crucial point, as noted in the Introduction, is that while producing or consuming discourse we be ever alert to what is going on.

The linguistic features you've studied in this book—and some others we didn't get to—comprise a **capacity profile** of the English language. They tell you what your language can and cannot do for you. In these remaining pages you will be introduced to an exciting new direction in language study which—due to its relative infancy—can only be exemplified here. This approach (actually older than Aristotle, but now newly scientific, with the anthropologists and the psychologists leading the way) seeks to discover the **impact of language limits and capacities on thought patterns.**

The words we think with

With the advent of computer science much recent attention has been directed toward language as an instrument of thought. Philosophers have for centuries pondered this elusive connection, with mixed results. But modern scientists agree that everyday syntax and vocabulary, suitable for most needs, cramp our thinking when a novel situation calls for departure from traditional patterns. We have already noted (in Chapter Four and elsewhere) the preponderance of property designators in the English language, blinding us to the relative nature of the world they describe. One remarkable example illustrates with a modern twist this phenomenon of language.

The language of motion and stillness. Most of us use words like "moving" and "stationary" without much trouble. Physical items are easily put into one category or the other: all one need do is look. In cases where it's hard to tell—as with a glacier—one at least knows **how** to measure the alleged movement. And to the language of motion we add designators of speed and direction. The result is a sub-set of motion symbols capable of describing certain aspects of the world we behold and, without our knowledge, telling us how to look at it and think about it.

An uneasy moment may brush us when, at a red traffic signal, our car seems to ease into the intersection. We quickly apply the brakes, only to learn that the car next to us had been coasting backward, giving the illusion that we were moving. We weren't **really** moving at all, we say with relief.

Then someone poses the question of the boy on the bus. If he roller-skates down the aisle toward the rear, at the same speed the bus is moving forward, is the boy moving or standing still? Here we are forced to alter our way of talking about motion—the boy is moving, we say, with respect to the bus, but is stationary with respect to the earth beneath. In spite of the relational "with respect to," however, we still cling to the idea of motion as a property; the boy-on-bus riddle was just a trick to confuse us.

Our property-oriented language gets a real jolt when someone re-vives the hunter-and-squirrel episode. It seems a hunter tries to shoot a squirrel, who scurries to the far side of a tree-trunk. As the hunter makes a full circle trying to get a shot, the squirrel circles also, wisely keeping the tree-trunk between him and the hunter. **Question:** Con-ceding that the hunter went around the tree, did he also go around the squirrel?

Most lay thinkers attack this riddle vigorously, picking a "yes" or a "no" answer and defending it. A more sophisticated response is that it depends on what you mean by "go around." If you mean "circum-scribe," the hunter did indeed go around the squirrel. If you mean "successively be exposed to all aspects of . . . ," the hunter did not go around the squirrel; for (even forgetting the tree) he was never exposed to the squirrel's back. But this latter answer requires accept-ance of a new notion—that "around" works only in certain neighbor-hoods. Again, the relative nature of motion forces itself upon our comfortable property-oriented language and thought.

With generation after generation talking and thinking this way it should come as no surprise that, in some quarters, the assertion that the earth is spherical still provokes the question, "Why don't the people on the under side fall off?" Even we who know better would probably be content with our earthbound syntax and vocabulary of motion, were it not for the intrusion of outer space. There, the convenient earth-center is no longer with us; and new linguistic habits are called for. Hundreds of words and phrases are useless, or must be redefined. Here are just a few:

moves	turns
rotates	upside down
under (over)	horizontal (vertical)
direction	reverse
falls (verb)	erect
drop	lie down
accelerate	elevator

The point is, not that new environment calls for new meanings, but that the meanings of these designators were seldom fully understood in the first place! Centuries of property language and property thinking had numbed us to the fact that each of these listed predicators is in some way tied to Mother Earth. For centuries we got away with a false assumption—that motion and stillness are properties of objects rather than relations among them.

Our little sojourn into the language of motion has merely exemplified how the words you think with control the distance and direction your thinking can go. Physical scientists have been able to outspeed our self-imposed linguistic limits; their science has leapt forward almost faster than traditional language can record. Now your generation is called on to make equal strides in the sciences of man. This perennial task requires a lot of talk; and only one language is handy. Even if you invent a new one, your fellows will have none of it. You must make do with what you have.

But it is, all in all, a good language. It is at least as good as we are; and often it speaks more clearly than we can think. For your workaday jobs it will serve you well. Knowing what you now know about language—its little quirks, its cranky habits, its great variety and wealth built out of inherent poverty—you will need no other. For you who look beyond pedestrian prose to the sounding of a higher note, your language will be ready—when you are.

Selected bibliography

Alexander, Hubert G. **Language and Thinking: A Philosophical Introduction.** Princeton, N. J.: D. Van Nostrand Company, Inc., 1967.

Austin, J. L. **How To Do Things with Words: The William James Lectures Delivered at Harvard University in 1955.** Cambridge, Mass.:
Harvard University Press, 1962.

Black, Max. **Critical Thinking: An Introduction to Logic and Scientific
Method.** New York: Prentice-Hall, Inc., 1946.

————, **Language and Philosophy: Studies in Method.** Ithaca, N. Y.:
Cornell University Press, 1949.

Brown, Roger. **Words and Things.** Glencoe, Ill.: The Free Press, 1958.

Hayakawa, S. I. **Language in Thought and Action.** 2nd ed. New York:
Harcourt, Brace and World, Inc., 1964.

Hall, Roland. "Excluders," **Analysis,** 20 (1959), 1-7.

Hughes, John. **The Science of Language: An Introduction to Linguistics.** New York: Random House, 1962.

Lee, Irving. "General Semantics," **Etc.,** IX, No. 2 (1952).

Orwell, George. **1984.** New York: Harcourt, Brace and Co., 1949.

Osgood, Charles E.; Suci, George J.; and Tannenbaum, Percy H., **The
Measurement of Meaning.** Urbana, Ill.: University of Illinois Press,
1957.

Shannon, Claude E.; and Weaver, Warren. **The Mathematical Theory of
Communication.** Urbana, Ill.: The University of Illinois Press, 1964.

Tillich, Paul. **Dynamics of Faith.** New York: Harper Torchbooks/The Cloister Library, of Harper & Row, Publishers.

Toulmin, S. E.; and Baier, H., "On Describing," **Mind,** LXI (1952), 13-38.

Whitehead, Alfred North; and Russell, Bertrand. **Principia Mathematica.** 2nd ed. Cambridge: The University Press, 1925.

Wellman, Carl. **The Language of Ethics.** Cambridge, Mass.: Harvard University Press, 1961.

Index

107